JUDSON PRESS

PUBLISHERS SINCE 1824

nuChristian

finding faith
in a new generation

RUSSELL E. D. RATHBUN

Foreword by Shane Claiborne

JUDSON PRESS
PUBLISHERS SINCE 1824
VALLEY FORGE, PA

nuChristian: Finding Faith in a New Generation

The author and Judson Press have made every effort to trace the ownership of all quotes. In the event of a question arising from the use of a quote, we regret any error made and will be pleased to make the necessary correction in future printings and editions of this book.

Bible quotations in this volume are from the New Revised Standard Version Bible, copyright 1989, Division of Christian Education of the National Council of the Churches of Christ in the United States of America. Used by permission. All rights reserved.

Library of Congress Cataloging-in-Publication Data
Rathbun, Russell. NuChristian: finding faith in a new generation/Russell E.D. Rathbun; foreword by Shane Claiborne. — 1st ed.
p. cm.
ISBN 978-0-8170-1549-7 (pbk.: alk. paper) 1. Church work with youth—United States. 2. Kinnaman, David, 1973- UnChristian. 3. Christianity—United States—Public opinion. 4. Youth—United States—Attitudes. 5. Public opinion—United States. I. Title.
BV4447.R358 2009
259'.23—dc22   2009027216

Printed in the U.S.A.
First Edition, 2009.

contents

Foreword

There is a new kind of Christianity emerging from the compost of Christendom. It is a Christianity that is rapidly changing the stereotypes of evangelicalism—away from being anti-gay, judgmental, and hypocritical and toward qualities such as grace, compassion, and justice.

It is a Christianity that is broadening the political agenda beyond the old hot button issues and stale debates toward the matters that Jesus had so much to say about—such as the poor and the peacemakers, the widows and the orphans. It is a Christianity that is creating new headlines—no longer just about cover-up bishops, abortion-clinic bombers, and embezzling televangelists but about a generation of Christians committed to ending poverty, exploitation, environmental degradation, militarism, and materialism.

The funny thing is that this new kind of Christian looks a lot like the Christians of old, the believers of the early church. It is a Christianity so old that it's new again.

I am convinced that if we lose a generation in the church, that loss won't be because we failed to entertain them, but because we failed to dare them—to take the words of Jesus seriously and to do something about the things that are wrong in the world. Russell Rathbun offers us that dare—to renew a Christianity that reminds the world of Jesus again.

—Shane Claiborne
author, activist, recovering sinner
www.thesimpleway.org

Preface

In 2007, David Kinnaman and Gabe Lyons published *unChristian*, an important book on what non-Christians in their late teens to early thirties think about Christians in general (Baker Books). The book is the result of a three-year study, and the findings are not flattering. The authors conclude that Christianity has an image problem that is affecting the ability to attract this younger generation. Of all the criticisms leveled by the study's respondents, Kinnaman and Lyons focus on six: Christians are only interested in "saving souls;" they are hypocritical, anti-homosexual, sheltered, too political, and judgmental.

In the final chapter of the book, Kinnaman writes, "Gabe and I hope this book generates ample conversation about the nature of and solutions for the slipping reputation of Christianity in our culture" (*unChristian*, p. 205). My intent is to join the conversation, a conversation that has been going on all over the place, from coffee shops and Bible studies to books and forums on websites like emergentvillage.com and theooze.com.

I want to take my small contribution to the conversation in a particular direction. Conversations are not like academic papers or logical equations; they speed up and slow down; they veer left and right; you say something, and it makes me think of something else that might be directly related to what you are talking about but also might be off-topic a little bit. Everyone in a conversation moves the discourse around. It is in this spirit that I write. Reading *unChristian* has led me to think about the issues I discuss in this book.

I hope that this book will be a constructive addition to the conversation and might serve to generate further discussion about how we proclaim the Good News of Jesus Christ in a way that doesn't sound like bad news to those who hear it. I am not thinking about the new generations, or postmoderns, from the point of view of objective research. I'm not built that way. I am a pastor, a preacher. I am reflecting on my experiences with people in that age group and with people from other age groups. I am incorporating what I have learned from people in my church and in other churches, from people I know who are not Christian and from what I read and hear and watch. So I write from a highly subjective, extremely relational perspective.

Non-Christian, unChristian, nuChristian

When non-Christians observe that the lives of Christians look a lot like the lives of people who are not Christians, they are right. Christians' lives look very similar to the lives of non-Christians. They look like human lives: messy, hypocritical, self-interested, judgmental, and competitive. But like all humans, Christians are also loving, compassionate, vulnerable, hopeful, and seeking relationship.

I hope we will begin to understand, as I continue this conversation, that it is more important to seek an authentic relationship with God and authentic relationships with all sorts of people—with those who are like us as well as with those who are not like us (whether in generation, race, belief, politics, or sexual orientation)—than it is to worry about God's reputation or our own. Repeatedly throughout our Holy Book, we encounter men and women whose lives are messy, hypocritical, self-interested, judgmental, and competitive, but they are also authentic, loving, compassionate, engaged, vulnerable, hopeful, humble, and seeking relationship.

In the first chapter, I hope to talk about some possible motivations for our concern with generational differences and with differences in general. I look at how easily we make the *other* into a scapegoat when we are challenged by beliefs, values, or ways of life that we do not agree with or understand. I explore how the life and work of Jesus Christ provides a way into relationship with the other person that is based on vulnerability and sacrifice, especially as this applies to the Mosaics and the Busters, the postmodern generations.

Chapter 2 begins a conversation about, how we actually know what a Christian is. I suggest that we know primarily through the Bible's witness to Jesus Christ. I also spend some time talking about how I read the Bible as a pastor and preacher of the Buster generation. There are several different terms that identify the generations that follow the Baby Boomers (generally understood as those born between 1946 and 1960 and the massive increase in the birthrate following World War II)—including Busters (referring to the comparative decrease in the birthrate following the Boomers), the 13th Generation (being the thirteenth generation since the founding of the United States), and Generation X or Gen X (this taken from the title of the seminal novel by Douglas Coupland, describing the zeitgeist of the cohort, which he took from the name of an English punk rock band).

This generation is defined by William Strauss and Neil Howe in their book *Generations: The History of America's Future* (Harper Perennial 1992), as those born between 1961 and 1981 and were often compared negatively to the generations that came before them. I also refer to the postmoderns or the postmodern generations, because this identifies them as coming of age entirely within the postmodern period, a time dating from the middle of the twentieth century to the present, and was first marked by the radical rethinking in the fields of literature, art, architecture, science, and religion. The terms postmoderns and postmodern generation is useful because it includes the generation that follows the Busters, generally known as the Mosaics in evangelical Christian circles (the term having been coined by evangelical author and researcher George Barna, for whose research organization, the Barna Group, *unChristian* author David Kinnaman works). Most demographers refer to this generation as Generation Y (because it follows Generation X) or the Millennials (given that they were born around the turn of the millennium). I most often use the phrase Busters and Mosaics, because those are the terms Kinnaman and Lyons use, in addition to postmoderns and the new generations, indicating the Busters and the Mosaics. In labeling any generation for study, it is important to keep in mind that the date ranges that identify them are fluid and approximate, realizing that individuals might identify with characteristics of a certain generation outside their age range. Also, when I make general statements in this book, saying, "Postmoderns think this way, or like this thing," these are of course generalizations, and I don't think that all people in a certain age range believe or think or like the exact same things.

In chapters 3 through 7, I weigh in on each of the six charges Kinnaman and Lyons focused on, devoting a chapter to each (with the exception of *anti-homosexual* and *judgmental,* which I address together). I ground each of these conversations in biblical stories of significant people who exhibited these unchristian qualities but were nonetheless loved, called, and used by God.

Throughout, I hope to move the conversation in a direction that relies on the transforming mercy of Jesus Christ, to compel Christians to enter into relationships with people of the Buster and Mosaic generations, so that we might walk with them as God works in their lives. I further hope that we will begin to see the ways that our lives and our faith might be expanded and deepened through these relationships. The new generations have much to offer the church, as natives of our postmodern, digital, and diverse world. Their tendency to seek partnership over power and good questions over assumed answers, their comfort with ambiguity and uncertainty, and their desire for relationship are all qualities that are reflected in the gospel. As we move into this conversation—and hopefully are encouraged to move into new conversations—I am confident that we will find a budding, authentic faith in these new generations, and that our faith will deepen as a result.

The struggle to change from bad Christian to good Christian seems like it is one dependent on the ability of individuals to behave better. In my experience and through my knowledge of history and the Bible, it is only through our transformation by God in Christ that we become the new creations we long to be. And that new creation (or should I say nucreation?) looks more like loving God and neighbor than it does being better behaved. So I accept the charge that my life looks unchristian, but I make the claim that through the action of Christ, I am a nuChristian.

A nuChristian does not seek moral or ethical perfection any more than he seeks to love perfectly of his own accord. A nuChristian understands that God not only loves her but likes her, not in spite of who she is but because of who she is, right now or at any given moment. A nuChristian accepts his humanity in all its faults and beauty but leaves judgment of self and others to God. A nuChristian seeks, above all, to love God with all that he is and to love his neighbor. Finally, a nuChristian knows she will do a lousy job at all of the above but has faith in the transforming love of Jesus Christ.

My contribution to this important conversation is only one voice, coming from the experience of a postmodern pastor and the House of Mercy, the postmodern church community I serve in St. Paul, Minnesota. I am sure my experiences will be similar to some of your experiences and very different from others. Perhaps this is an opportunity to meet the Other. And together we can explore what it might mean to be a nuChristian.

CHAPTER 1

Another Generation Gap

I want you to imagine yourself sitting in your regular weekly worship service. Is it Sunday? Is it morning or evening? Are you sitting on a pew, in a chair, on a couch, or on a pillow on the floor? Now look around. Whom do you see? Do you know most everyone there? What is the age range of the people you see? Are they younger than you, older than you, about the same age? Is there a broad range of ages? Do they talk like you, speaking the same language and sharing the same vocabulary? Do they look like they might come from the same neighborhood as you? Do they look like they might be in the same tax bracket as you? Can you guess if they have about the same degree of education as you do? Are they the same race as you? Or is there diversity in incomes, levels of education, and cultures?

Most churches I visit have a very narrow demographic range. That is, most people look the same and have similar life experiences. It is a simple reality that most people feel more comfortable with people like themselves. This realization has even been put to use as a strategy in starting and growing churches. Called the *"homogenous unit principle"*, it was introduced by Donald A. McGavran as a core principle in the church growth movement, a movement associated with Fuller Seminary in Pasadena, California, which arose in the early 1960s and relies heavily on social and behavioral science to understand the factors that facilitate or hinder church growth.

The idea is that when someone walks into a church and sees a bunch of people just like himself or herself—same age, same race, even dressed the same—he or she immediately feels more comfortable and is more likely to stick around. And you know what? The idea really works.

I'm one of the pastors at a church called House of Mercy in St. Paul, Minnesota. When we started the church, most of us were in our twenties and had no kids. We were a decidedly white, decidedly urban group. We were college graduates, quite a few with advanced degrees. A lot of us were really into art and music. A great majority of us had not regularly attended church in the previous year before finding House of Mercy. I realize this is not a description that would fit the majority of American churches, but that was what visitors to the House of Mercy liked about us. People "like us" were surprised to find a church made up of people almost entirely "like them." Community members would bring their friends, and a lot of those friends kept coming back. However, those who were even a little bit older than we were and had kids would sometimes tell us that they didn't feel comfortable or that there was not a place for them and their kids at House of Mercy. I say "sometimes" people would tell us, because mostly they didn't say anything; they just never came back.

Almost fourteen years later, if you were to walk through the doors of our church and into the gathering space outside the sanctuary (we call it the Den of Mercy), you will see dozens of kids running around, parents chasing them or trying to have conversations while their six-year-olds pull at them. There is a play area set up for the toddlers, and you can even find a small group of teenagers slumped on one of the couches checking out Miles's iPod or Oden's Nintendo DS.

Recently, we have been getting comments from people who are in their twenties with no kids, saying that they wish there were more people like them at the House of Mercy. On the other hand, when young families visit the church, they tell us they feel at home and are glad there are other children the same age as their own. It doesn't mean we don't try to meet the needs of those twenty-year-olds now or that, fourteen years ago, we didn't work to make connections with the young families with kids.

It seems to be a basic truth: We feel more comfortable with people who are like us. Another part of that basic truth is that people tend to avoid uncomfortable situations. This leads to most churches being made up of very similar groups of people.

The kingdom of God doesn't use the homogenous unit principle. The kingdom of God is made up of every kind of person there is. Breaking down barriers and expanding the circle of God's kingdom is part of the mission of the Christian church. Most churches realize this and would never try to build a community that would exclude anyone. Many churches hold diversity as a core value, seeking to reflect the kingdom of God in their congregations. Here is where the homogenous unit principle becomes a challenge, a hindrance to the kind of deep growth healthy churches need, and the principle can lead to some unwanted results.

Let's say there is a church community that started about sixty years ago, after the end of World War II. At that time, lots of couples were getting married, were buying their first houses in the first-ring suburbs, and were starting families. So a new church was really needed in that first-ring suburb. Let's call the town Maplebrook, because that sounds like a first-ring-suburb name, and it is more fun to imagine things when they have names. A young couple, Bob and Betty Jaworski, buy a new house, a cute little rambler in Maplebrook. Betty is already five months pregnant, and they are looking for a church. They have driven by the brand-new Maplebrook church and decide to check it out one Sunday. They walk in the door, and what do they see? Other young couples. Betty counts five other pregnant women right away. "It is almost like some kind of baby boom," Betty says to Bob.

The Jaworskis find a real home at the Maplebrook church. They have more kids; they serve on boards and help with the youth group; they attend all-church dinners and Bible studies. It's all great fun, and they do this for the next twenty years or so. As their families grow up and begin to leave home, Betty and Bob and Sue and Bart and the other leaders of the church realize that the kids also seem to be leaving the church. As a matter of fact, it seems like an entire generation is leaving the church. As the years go by, the good people at the Maplebrook church feel as if they have a real problem on their hands.

How could it be that their own children don't love their church in the same way as the parents always have? How could this church that means so much to Bob and Betty not mean just as much to young Bobby and Betts? The Jaworskis and their peers wonder if they have done something wrong, if they have failed to teach the children something important. They wonder what is wrong with the whole younger generation. They can't even understand these kids: the music they listen to, the way they dress, the books they read. And worst of all, they can't believe what their children believe—or *don't* believe. The kids seem to be questioning everything. They are not only questioning what they were taught in church, they are questioning the government, even protesting a war while American soldiers are in a far-off country risking their lives. While the Jaworskis hold out some hope that Bobby Jr. and Betts are still Christians and will come back to the church one day, they think that most of the younger generation has rejected Christianity and seems to be pursuing "unchristian" or "New Age" religious practices, like meditation and living in communes. This lost generation seems to care more about their own pleasure than anything else. So the good people at the Maplebrook church form a committee to try and figure out what to do about *those* people.

The committee talks about the issue, but it is not completely clear what the problem is—or maybe there are several. This new generation is not going to church, is questioning Christianity, and is questioning their parents—good, churchgoing Christians. The Jaworskis and their peers think, *They* are judging *us* for believing what is true. If *they* don't ever come back to Christianity, what is going to happen to *them*? If *they* don't come back to church, what is going to happen to *us*? The church will die when we do.

I know that scenario seems a little far-fetched, a bit exaggerated, but remember we are imagining. So, how about going a little further with me?

"Making the Different the *Other*"

There are some theologians, anthropologists, and cultural observers who would say there is a theory at the heart of the Maplebrook church scenario, a theory as old as human culture. James Alison, a contemporary British Catholic theologian, is one of them, and this is what he taught me: We learn to be who we are by imitating the people in our lives. This is how we learn to walk and talk. This is how we learn to feel and learn what to value. It is how we learn what we understand to be right or wrong. This is just one theory about these issues. There are, of course, other, more popular theories, but let's stick with the pretending and pretend we know this theory is truth for just a while.

If we become who we are by imitating other people, the theory goes, then we learn what we want—James Alison uses the word *desire*—by imitating others. We learn what we desire by seeing what other people desire. We want what other people want or what other people have.

Now, when we encounter people who have learned to want something different from us, because they have grown up imitating a different group of people or have had different life experiences than we have had, we are either threatened by that difference or are envious of who they are or what they have. This causes inner conflict and rivalry. We ask ourselves all kinds of questions, either consciously or not: Is there something wrong with the way I am? Should I be more like them? Do they think they are better than me? In order to deal with that conflict, we engage in what James Alison and his contemporaries call *scapegoating*. Scapegoating is when we find someone else like us, and we bond over the shared object of our envy, anxiety, or fear.

Perhaps the good people at Maplebrook looked at the young generation—whose parents didn't understand and had a kind of freedom that their parents couldn't imagine—and felt an unclear mixture of thoughts and feelings of which the parents themselves were not consciously aware. Maybe they felt envious of the youth, remembering a time when they were bold and full of all kinds of energies. Maybe the parents also felt like there were some things that the new generation knew that the parents should know, that the parents were behind the times or ignorant. Or perhaps they thought that if so many of the new generation questioned long-held beliefs, maybe those beliefs were wrong. Or they felt that the new generation had abandoned the truth of Christianity and were a threat to their faith and way of life. Of course, they also felt that these kids were lost and needed the saving love of Jesus so that they might know truth and happiness.

That is a lot going on unconsciously, consciously, or semiconsciously. It is confusing and causes profound inner conflict or distortion of desire. Scapegoating is a reliable way to relieve that inner conflict. Scapegoating, or creating a common enemy, works wonders when you're trying to feel okay about yourself. Scapegoating is the mechanism of making the person or persons we are in conflict with somehow seem bad or separate from us, worse than us—an outsider, the *Other*. Groups do this as well as individuals. On a group level, we make them into *Them*.

The Conflict of Desires

Which brings me back to the Maplebrook church and their problem with the new generation. Here is a possible way to understand the scenario:

The new generations do not desire what Bob and Betty's generation desires. They have learned to want some slightly different things. The founders of the Maplebrook church wanted the stability that they found in organizations and traditions of faith. The new generations desire the freedom that comes from questioning organizations and traditions; they want to do their own thing their own way.

There is a conflict in desires going on here. On the one hand, the next generation does not desire what *we* desire, so that calls into question what we desire. It is hard to ask ourselves if we might be wrong or if there is something they know that we do not know. If we do not want the same thing, then one of us must be wrong. We don't believe, of course, that the one in the wrong is *us*. That would be fine, but the fact that *they* think we are wrong threatens us, so we have to make them somehow wrong—by making them the Other, the outsiders.

This scapegoating concept certainly doesn't just apply to churches. It's alive in every area of our lives. It's how political alliances are formed, how political parties work. It is how a nation finds itself at war. Those people are different from us; they don't share our values; they must hate freedom, so we have to defend ourselves against those others. It is the most human response to conflict. And it is also in direct opposition to the Good News of Jesus Christ. Throughout the New Testament, we find a consistent message of reaching out to the other, of engaging those who are different from us, of breaking down barriers.

It is with these realities in mind—we are natural scapegoating machines by virtue of the fact that we're human, and the scapegoating mechanism is in opposition to the core message of our faith—that I want to move forward in exploring the charges that Christians, in the eyes of those in the new generations, appear to act more like non-Christians.

The Lifespan of a Church

Is the experience that the Maplebrook church went through simply the same experience that comes with every generational shift? The founding generation grows older raises their children. The children begin to separate from their parents, to question their parents, and to have different experiences as the ever-changing culture presents them with different ideas and possibilities. And if so, is that what is at the heart of the way today's younger generations see the Christian church?

There is the sort of general belief that a church is an institution that has a long, long history and, therefore, should have a long, long future. There are historic churches that have been around in this country for several hundred years, and in Europe a few that have been there for five hundred years. I remember hearing in a seminary class on evangelism that the average period that most churches could be considered thriving was about sixty years. This is just long enough for young, energetic believers to question their parents' understanding of what church should be, band together and form a new church, grow that church and grow up in that church together, get married there, have and raise children, see their children grow up and leave, retire and play golf together, and then die and be buried in the churchyard. The average life of a church is about the time it takes one generation to live their lives together as an expression of the body of Christ. I think this is a beautiful thing. It should not be mourned but celebrated. Christianity is a dynamic faith, a moving faith. Jesus is always on a journey, always moving. In the Old Testament, the patriarchs are always moving; God called Israel out of Egypt through the desert. It sometimes seems that when the people of God stop moving and start growing and putting down roots, things begin to stagnate. In the arc of history, God's ability to reconcile the world to God's self will not be hindered if the Maplebrook church closes its doors because their children go off and start something new. In the same way, God's plan will not be hindered if the House of Mercy closes its doors.

It's interesting to realize that the generation that our fictional friends at the Maplebrook church were so worried about is responsible for the most significant phenomenon in American Christianity in the second half of the twentieth century. They are the Baby Boomer generation, who dropped out of the church, returned in large numbers, and found new ways to express their faith. They got rid of the organs and brought in the guitars and started up the praise bands and applied cutting-edge marketing and networking principles to create the ascendancy of the evangelical movement. They made Christianity relevant to American culture in a way that it hadn't been in quite some time.

Are today's younger generations, who are finding fault with the way Christianity currently looks, possibly the foundation of the next significant movement in American Christianity? I think so. In fact, that movement has already started. These new generations are very different from the Baby Boomer generation and the generations that came before them. In some ways, the so-called postmodern generations are different from preceding generations in the same ways all generations experience a "gap," but I believe there is also something more going on, that a more significant shift has occurred.

There Really Is Such a Thing as Postmodernity

These new generations are the first to come of age and live their lives entirely in the postmodern period. *Postmodernity* can be most succinctly described as this time period that lacks any common foundational assumptions or metanarratives. There is no one overarching system, idea, or belief that is appealed to, to understand

and explain all things. In premodern times, God or a god was seen as the ground of all things. It rained because God made it rain, and the rain probably meant God was pleased with you. If it didn't rain, that was because God stopped it from raining, which probably meant that you had done something to make God mad. If you wanted answers to some philosophical or scientific question, you started with God and reasoned from there.

Eventually people began to make observations and reason their way to answers that had nothing to do with God. In the modern period, reason was the common foundational assumption. All things could be known, explained, and figured out using reason. Then people began to notice that what they thought was objective reasoning was really dependent on who they were, where they were, and what they had been exposed to. Things looked different and were different, depending on who was looking at them.

This, in my very oversimplified version of intellectual and cultural history, leads us to the postmodern period in which we now live, where there is no common foundational assumption. Many different people, from many different places, make many different assumptions when they ask questions about God and science and faith and art. The ramifications of this are, of course, many. And as this important shift in thinking has moved out of the realm of academics and the arts into the popular culture, it has had an effect on the culture, which can be seen clearly in the younger generations.

In the following chapters, I will touch on how the postmodern generations interact with the culture, the Bible, faith, God, each other, institutions, politics, and ethics.

Making the Other *Us*

Remember when I asked you to close your eyes and you pretended to be in your church, in the primary worship service? I asked you to look around and note all of the people there. Did you see a diverse group of people? Did you see a lot of people that were different than you? If you didn't, it is not unusual. It's what most churches look like. It's what most restaurants, bars, movie theaters, bookstores, and health clubs look like. Of course, the church is an expression of the body of Christ, a living expression of the kingdom of God, so hopefully, it should look like a more inclusive group of people than you would find in a restaurant or theater or health club. But while the church is an expression of the body of Christ, it is also a reflection of the culture. It is both things simultaneously, and when our churches begin to resemble the kingdom of God more than they resemble our culture, even in just the tiniest ways, we can praise God for the ways in which we are being transformed through Christ. And when our churches are exact mirrors of our culture, what do we do? We go meet the other, search for the outsider.

Let's go meet the new generations. Because when we encounter people who are different from us and invite them into relationships, we will see that we have things to learn from each other. We will feel that we are more alike than we are different. We will see that we are all made in the image of God for relationship, made to love God and to love our neighbors. Then we begin to see how we can move from seeing the *other* to seeing *us;* we begin to understand what the kingdom of God could look like.

CHAPTER 2

How Do We Know
What It Means to Be a Christian?

In the face of the charge that many Christians are, in fact, living lives that could be called unchristian, I'd like to spend some time with the question: How do we know what it means to be a Christian?

We all learn what it means to be a Christian from other Christians. For many of us, those other Christians are our families, our mothers and fathers, our grandmothers and grandfathers. We are *taught* what it means to be a Christian, and those lessons come in many forms. First and primarily, it is through observation, which is of course how we learn most things at a young age. When I recall the things I observed as a little kid that taught me about being a Christian, the first lesson I learned was that Christians go to church. My dad is a Baptist preacher, so maybe I learned that lesson a lot more thoroughly than other people might have.

I also learned that it was a *good* thing to be a Christian. It seemed like my mom and dad and grandmas and grandpas and a lot of people at church really liked being Christians. It seemed like a good thing and the right thing to be a Christian. I didn't grow up with a lot of heavy strictures. The Christianity that was modeled for me didn't have a lot of heavy-handed "thou shalt nots." I never got messages such as Christians don't dance; Christians don't listen to a certain kind of music; Christians don't hang around with disreputable people. The opposite was true. Our church and our lives were filled with all kinds of music and arts, with people making candles and sculptures in the church basement. And disreputable people? They were everywhere. Well, so-called disreputable people. I know this is not the kind of formative church experience that most evangelicals had, but it was mine, and I loved it.

I realized early on that Christians didn't go to church a lot just to be in that building. Christians went to church to be together. One thing being a Christian is about is people—people being together, studying together, singing together, experiencing pain together, praying together, playing together, loving each other, helping each other, and sacrificing for each other. The idea that a Christian is someone who will sacrifice himself, whether that means putting someone else's desires before his own or even risking his safety for someone else's was modeled for me time and time again by my dad.

I remember one time we were driving home from our after-church-going-out-to-eat at Country Kitchen when we saw a long-haired, bearded, gigantic man. He looked like a biker, and he had ahold of this skinny woman and was shaking her violently from side to side. The next thing he did surprised and shocked me: he pulled back his left hand and punched her right in the face. She dropped to the ground like a rag doll. My heart was pounding. The next thing that happened made my heart pound even faster. My dad slammed on the brakes pulled to the side of the road and before the car had even fully stopped, he jumped out of the car, ran to the sidewalk, and stepped between the man and the woman just as the man was moving to grab her again. My dad put his hands on the giant's shoulders and told him to stop. My mom told us to close our eyes. I am sure she was thinking what my brothers and sister and I were thinking: our dad was about to get killed. But I was never the kind of person who would close my eyes in the face of fear or violence. The guy shoved my dad back and started swearing at him. And instead of preparing for a fight or to defend himself, Dad simply turned his back on the man and knelt down to help the woman. Then he turned back to the man and said, "You had better leave now, or I'll call the police." The giant made one more feint with his left hand, cursed the woman, turned, and left. My dad helped her into the car, talked to her, and asked her if she had a place to go. "No. No place," she said. And that is how Kelly ended up living with us for the next year. Kelly was neither the first nor the last person to stay in that bedroom in our basement. There were always people who needed help, who had no options, and my parents brought them in. It was clear to me that my parents did this because they were Christians, and that's what Christians do.

Listening, Learning, and Reading the Bible

Another thing I learned by observation was that Christians read the Bible. Again, not everybody's experience is the same. There are traditions other than my Baptist evangelical upbringing where the Bible isn't around as much. In our case, the Bible was everywhere. There was a Bible on a bookshelf in every room. My dad read it in the morning. My mom read it on the living room couch. The way they pored over it, even the way they held it, made it seem like it was a really important book. The height of the Sunday worship service was all about the sermon, which was all about interpreting the Bible. In Sunday school, we learned Bible stories. We learned how to navigate the Bible, where the different books were. We learned the differences between the Old Testament and the New Testament and the differences among the Gospels, Acts, and the Epistles. We learned about Peter, the fisherman, and about Jesus walking on water, and about there being no room at the inn. We learned about John 3:16. We learned how Nicodemus came at night, so he would not be seen by men, and how he asked Jesus what he must do to be saved. We learned how Jesus told him, "You must be born again."

Of course, I know that not everyone's understanding of what it means to be a Christian is the same as mine. People grow up in different families, in different kinds of subcultures, and in different kinds of denominational traditions. Some people grow up in fundamentalist families, where it seems like being a Christian is all about what you should and shouldn't do and the subsequent punishments and rewards for living out those proscriptions and admonitions. Other people grow up in traditions where being a Christian means trying to be a good person, and that is said with no greater exploration or consequence.

Another way we learn what it means to be a Christian is through what we are taught. We learn not just by observing what people do and what they hold important, but by listening to what they say. Sometimes we are taught in a formal setting like Sunday school, church services, or Bible studies, and sometimes we are taught in conversation, either casual or deliberate. We listen to our pastors, our teachers, our parents, and our peers.

I remember the first time the doctrine of the Trinity was laid out for me completely. I was seven, and I knew there was Jesus, and I knew there was God, and I knew there was the Holy Spirit. I had just never stopped to think about what they all had to do with each other. And then one day, at the end of Sunday school, while we had our graham cracker and grape juice snack, Maria Ferguson asked me, "Do you know who God is?" I said, "Um, yeah, I know who God is. Sure," not really understanding what she was getting at. She continued, "You see, there is only one God and that's God, but there's also God who made everything, and Jesus, and the Holy Spirit. And the Holy Spirit's name is Tom. And he's a girl. And they're all the same God, but they're all different people." And I remember thinking, "Wow," and kind of understanding what that meant, a little. And aside from the Holy Spirit being a girl named Tom, I think it was a remarkably succinct explanation of the doctrine of the Trinity, for a seven-year-old.

Which brings me to another way we learn what it means to be a Christian. We study. We read the Bible, and we read books about the Bible, and we read theology, which is how I learned for sure that the Holy Spirit is not a girl named Tom. Throughout our lives, this constant process of learning by observation, of listening, and of studying, the Holy Spirit is there, revealing things to us. Revelation is another way we learn, and it is frankly harder to nail down or to talk about, but the Holy Spirit is there.

Of all these ways that we learn what it means to be a Christian, however, the primary witness we have is our Holy Book, the Bible. So whatever we are taught, we can bring those understandings to the Bible and check them out, wrestle with them, and question them.

Christianity is one of the three great religions of the Book. Because our Holy Book is such a central part of our faith and our tradition, it has been read and interpreted by many different people over the last two thousand years. And of course, when you have different people in different cultures at different points in history interpreting the text, you end up with many different types of interpretation. In Europe in the Middle Ages, almost everything was read as an allegory. In the early part of the twentieth century in the United States, a group of people at Princeton University declared that every single word in the Bible should be taken literally. Christians in Central and South America in the early 1980s found in the New Testament a gospel of social and political liberation. Current academic interpreters of Scripture are reading the text in many exciting ways from many different social perspectives.

Postmoderns Read the Bible

In this postmodern age, many a Christian's relationship with the Bible is changing, especially among the younger generations. For previous generations, the Bible was popularly seen as an instruction book, a guidebook, a book of answers. This set of instructions and answers were meant to be studied, meditated on, and memorized. Postmodern interpreters, even within the evangelical movement, are beginning to question this sort of understanding of the Bible. If one accepts the notion that there is no overarching, single set of truths for everyone in every situation—as postmoderns do—then one would look for a more dynamic, transformational relationship with our Holy Book. To see the Bible as static and unchanging raises questions about the God to whom that Holy Book bears witness. To say that there is one right interpretation of every text in the Bible is to see the Scriptures as something dead. If something is alive, it is growing and changing, being affected by interactions with other people and texts. Of course the Bible is not actually changing, the words are not morphing and moving, but we are changing. If we have a faith that is alive, our understanding of the biblical witness will change and grow as we grow, mature, and learn.

In the past, people interpreted the Bible in ways that endorsed slavery and forbade women to serve in leadership positions in the church, but our growing understanding of the equality and value of each individual has changed the way those Scriptures are understood. The early church reinterpreted many of the Old Testament prophecies as referring to Jesus—obviously a way they had never been understood previously.

The ancient rabbis believed that every word in the Bible had an infinite amount of meanings and that all of them were partly right and partly wrong. We can learn something from every interpretation, when we set those interpretations next to each other, when they are in conversation with each other. Jesus read the Bible (the Old Testament) like a rabbi, often debating the meaning of particular Scriptures with the religious leaders. The Sermon on the Mount is largely the reinterpretation of passages from Leviticus and the Prophets. There are, of course, interpretations that emerge from these conversations over time that seem to be most helpful or edifying or give us a clearer glimpse of God's mercy, and those are the interpretations we usually think of as Christian orthodoxy. But that doesn't mean the conversation should end or that it isn't fruitful.

For today's younger generations, black-and-white distinctions rarely exist. But that doesn't mean that their world is made up of varying degrees of gray. No, both black and white are there, as are a rainbow of other colors, not blending together but sitting side by side, distinct from one another. Black looks a little different when set next to orange than it does when set next to yellow or purple or white, revealing a slightly different understanding and raising slightly different questions.

What if we looked at the Bible not as a book of answers, but as a book of really good questions? A book of the best questions about the nature of God, about who we really are, about how we relate to God, to each other, and to the natural world? It's the finding of these questions in the text and measuring them against the answers we've always thought we had in the context of our communities that makes our Holy Book alive, profound, and transformative.

If this all sounds like some kind of theological/biblical relativism, it really isn't. But I admit it is a very different way of seeing the Bible than a lot of us have been taught. So again, I ask you to just sit with it and consider it. I'm not asking you to accept it or reject it at this point, but just to try and understand it in the spirit that it is being offered. By saying the Bible is not a book of answers that are applicable for all people at all times, I am not devaluing its importance or its authority. By claiming the Bible as my Holy Book, I grant it great authority. And by claiming the Bible as our primary witness to Jesus Christ, I am granting it the utmost authority. By committing myself to an ongoing relationship with this Holy Book, in pursuit of the good news of the kingdom of God, I am taking it far more seriously than I would if I interpreted it literally.

This paradigm shift, from seeing the Bible as a book of answers to seeing it as a book of questions, is admittedly a hard one to make for most congregations. But I have found in my own ministry that highlighting the questions we find in the Scriptures gives people permission to voice the questions they have always wondered about. This questioning, in turn, leads to a deeper engagement with the Bible.

To only interpret the Bible literally and to say that I fully understand what the texts in the Bible mean can begin to create distance in my relationship with God. Because if I know this set of rules, I know what's right and wrong, what is righteous, and what is sin. I know what it means to love my neighbor. If I know who is good and who is bad, then I don't need God. I can just take that set of rules, put them on a chart up on the wall or make a spreadsheet, and then keep track of my behavior in the world. Did I take the Lord's name in vain? Yes. Check the box. Did I lust in my heart? Yes. Check the box. Did I enter the Lord's gates with thanksgiving in my heart? Yes. Check the box. Now all I have to do at the end of the day is add up all of my answers, and I can see if I was good or bad that day. You don't need a relationship when you have a checklist. You don't need God when you have a checklist. None of us really wants a checklist; we don't study the Scriptures to find a checklist. We study the Bible to learn more about the God we love, to learn more about who we are. The checklist just kind of seems to happen.

But what if, instead of a checklist, I had an ancient text that was written over a five-thousand-year period of time? A Holy Book that was written in three or four different cultural contexts, in three or four different languages? A Holy Book that was born out of people of faith passing down stories from mothers and fathers to sons and daughters, stories carried from Egypt and carried from Babylon? Stories and sayings of Jesus told and retold for forty years before someone wrote them down? And then, with all these stories written down, what if I had nearly two thousand years of people of faith trying to interpret and understand and live out what they had found in this Holy Book? All of this in the service of a people trying to understand how this God of creation and re-creation comes to us and transforms us in love, so that we might live full and abundant lives free from the powers of sin and evil, free from the power of death. Now that kind of book invites relationship. It requires me to invest myself and expose myself, to read on my knees in faith, and to gather others into this exciting pursuit.

Postmodern generations value complexity, rich content, and relationship. The Christian story, told and witnessed in the Bible, is the most complex, rich witness to the true meaning of what relationship is meant to be. The new generations already suspect and long for what our Holy Book bears witness to. We can learn from Mosaics and Busters a natural comfort level with questions, contradictions, and complexity. It is hard to see past what we have always understood a text to mean. We could benefit from a new set of eyes, from the new perspectives postmoderns can bring.

I believe we can know some very important things about what it means to be a Christian through reading the Bible in community, not only in our present communities, but also in the larger historic community of all those who have interpreted the text over time. When Debbie Blue and Mark Stenberg (our cofounders and friends) and I started House of Mercy, we agreed that at the core of everything we did, we would be proclaiming the mercy of God by pointing to Jesus Christ, and that our primary method for pointing to Jesus Christ would be the rigorous and passionate interpretation of the Scriptures. We would use the Good News as our interpretive rule. When we looked at a text, no matter how difficult or off-putting it was, we would believe that we could find the Good News in it.

Over the last fourteen years that House of Mercy has been in existence, preaching and Bible study have been the heart of our community, the heart where the desire and passion for what we do is born and nurtured.

I've been studying the Bible with the same core group of people every week for the last twelve years. Over the years, we've studied the Gospels three or four times, Paul's epistles, Revelation, the small epistles, Genesis, Exodus, the Prophets, and many more. We have approached these texts using every kind of biblical interpretive method imaginable. We've used narrative criticism and historical critical methods. We've delved into the historic social, political, and geographic contexts out of which the books arose. We've studied

> **What questions do you have about the Bible and about faith? How might exploration of those questions deepen your relationship with God and with God's people?**

the Pentateuch, using the ancient rabbis and postmodern literary critics and psychologists as our guides. We've used feminist, womanist, and Catholic liberation interpretive frameworks. We've studied the Bible alongside the works of theologians like Karl Barth, Martin Luther, Søren Kierkegaard, and even some contemporary evangelical theologians. We study eagerly and rigorously, believing always that this Holy Book that we have committed ourselves to, when read in community and read with integrity, would reveal to us the Good News of Jesus Christ. Our study has not always been done so easily or clearly and has caused many of us to question our faith in the midst of a deep morass of uncertainty. But miraculously, and I do not use the word lightly, in the end we were always drawn closer together and closer to God, who was the object of our study. Our relationship with one another and our relationship with God only deepened as a result of this approach to the Bible.

Erin and Jeremy Get Married

For most of those twelve years, this Bible study has been at the house of Erin and Jeremy, two postmodern generation youngsters. (I call them *youngsters,* but I think now they must be in their early thirties.) Erin and Jeremy came to the House of Mercy from very different places. Jeremy grew up as an evangelical. By the time he was in college, he'd stopped going to church altogether, disillusioned by the repeated messages of judgment and the demonization of the world and anyone who didn't share his church's same narrow beliefs. I met him while we were both serving on the planning board of the Lower Town Art Crawl in St. Paul.

When Erin came to the House of Mercy, she was an atheist. She had grown up in a liberal church, where she said she rarely ever heard them even mention Jesus. Early in her teens, she decided that the church and Christianity had nothing to offer her. Erin is really smart (she has an MBA with a focus on nonprofit organizations and has written several books on the subject), so she didn't just shrug her shoulders and throw faith out the window. She explored other religious traditions and organizations whose followers seek to live ethical lives and found interests that were meaningful to her, like working for social justice in education and helping the disenfranchised and those in poverty. She joined our Bible study about the same time Jeremy did. I don't know if she joined because Jeremy had—they had recently become friendly—but it was great that she decided to become a part of our group.

Their courtship played out over the course of several Bible Studies, and they were eventually married. It just so happened that shortly after they had bought a house, we were in need of a new place to hold the Bible study, and they offered to host. From then on, Bible study was always at Erin and Jeremy's house. Of course, while this is a beautiful, moving, heartwarming story about two people meeting, falling in love, and getting married, it is at the same time a story about something equally beautiful. Two people from these new generations, who had different experiences with two very different kinds of churches and who had rejected their childhood faiths, were able to find something in this intense study of the Bible that they didn't get in their childhood churches.

While Jeremy knew the Bible backward and forward, like most good evangelicals do, he heard new ideas in our Bible study, ideas that transformed him and the way he lived his life. When Erin joined the Bible study, she said she'd never read the Bible before in her life. But because she was encountering Scripture for the first time, bringing with her not a lifetime of hearing the same simple interpretations of the text over and over, but an inquisitive mind and an education that had taught her how to read closely and to ask real questions, she found something new. Too many times to count, Erin has found ideas in the Scriptures we study that none of the rest of us have noticed. She's become one of the best interpreters of Scripture I know. Like Jeremy, she too says that the Bible study has changed the way she lives her life, does her job, and interacts with other people.

I know it may seem counterintuitive, when thinking about ways to attract and engage these new generations, for me to recommend biblical preaching and Bible study, but I don't know how to do it any other way. Not with integrity.

Jesus Loves Me, This I Know, for the Bible Tells Me So

I think the postmoderns who are attracted to House of Mercy come in large part because the Bible is so out front. We put what we are about and what is important to us out in front. There are no hidden agendas. Every week we seek to proclaim the Good News of Jesus Christ through the interpretation of Scripture and the gift of communion. But we do it with honesty about our struggles and doubts. We don't shrink from the Scriptures that speak a hard word or that seem difficult. We are not there to defend the Bible or God or Jesus, not even the Holy Spirit. They need no defense; they can take anything we throw at them—questions, doubts, anger, or befuddlement.

How do we know what it means to be a Christian? We know that the Bible bears witness to Christ, and by engaging the Bible in a relational, transformative way, we can be on that journey to discovering what it means to be a Christian. That doesn't mean we can never be assured of anything, if we take our assurance in the form of faith. The entire arc of our Holy Book, from Genesis to Revelation, tells the story of God who creates in love, desires relationship with his creation, and pursues us through history, so that we might be reconciled to Him, freed to live in love with our neighbor and to live life fully and abundantly in the presence of the One who loves us completely.

That means we can answer the question, "What does it mean to be a Christian?" like this: Christianity is all about Christ. God is in

Christ, reconciling the world to God's self. It is Christ who pursues us. It is Christ who is the embodiment of love, the Author of life, the Redeemer from death, the Reconciler of all, through God's judgment and mercy.

Being a Christian isn't about who we are, but about who Christ is. That is, Christ is our Redeemer and the Author of the transforming love we seek to reflect as we live our lives. When we struggle honestly with what this means and how it can compel us to live our lives, those new generations who are barraged daily with deception and hollow content in the service of the hidden agendas of marketers, manipulators, and cultural power players, will recognize that they have stumbled onto something real. Even if that real truth requires us to confess our falseness and lies, those confessions are necessary if we are to invite non-Christian postmoderns to engage in this beautiful pursuit with us. They will understand that we don't want to do anything to them judge them or force them to believe anything, but that we desire above all else to be in relationship with them.

■ nuChristians don't defend the Bible or see it as a book of definitions or a book of rules or a checklist of righteousness, but engage it in a relational and transformational way.

■ nuChristians see the Bible as the witness to the Word of God, who is Jesus the Christ.

■ nuChristians understand that new questions are a sign of new growth.

■ nuChristians engage the Bible in relationship with others, both in their current community context and in the historic community of interpreters over time.

■ nuChristians understand that being a nuChristian is all about being a new creation in Christ.

■ nuChristians know that being a Christian is the only way to know what a Christian is.

CHAPTER 3

Can We Practice What We Preach?
nuChristians and Authenticity

"All of them deserted him and fled"
(Mark 14:50).

Hypocrisy and You

It is hard for me to imagine people I know, Christians and non-Christians, using the word *hypocrite* in everyday conversation. It is such an old word. It sounds outdated. Not that the concept is outdated, but it is more likely to be talked about in terms of authenticity. New generations are actually very concerned with authenticity. They take for granted the omnipresence of marketing. Nearly everything they encounter in our culture is a product of some kind, and because marketing concepts are so ingrained in the younger generations' way of thinking, advertisers have become increasingly aware that they need many and varied ways to communicate to the new generations. Advertisers use aspirational marketing, lifestyle marketing, green marketing, relational marketing, transformational marketing, ambient intimacy marketing, and on and on. Not only are many in the new generations familiar with these marketing strategies, but they are comfortable using them to promote themselves on social networking sites like Facebook. People in this age group are very aware of their own images and are deliberate in the way they present themselves.

In a culture where everything, even every individual, is a product to be positioned or marketed, authenticity is rare and sought after. In conversations, I do hear people using words like *fake*, *plastic*, and *affected*. And they don't want fake. They don't want fake food, fake clothes, fake people, fake ideas, and certainly not fake faith.

A Big Bible Hypocrite

Mark's story of Jesus is a great one for Christians and non-Christians—for hypocrites. The secondary, sidekick character in Mark's gospel is Peter. Peter is known as the founder of the church. In the book of Acts, he seems to be running things, but from Mark's account, Peter always had that tendency. He puts himself out there; he steps up; he is a get-'er-done kind of guy. He is bold in his action and bold in his pronouncements. He is the kind of guy who is practically setting himself up for the charge: *hypocrite*.

We meet Peter sixteen verses into the first chapter of the Gospel. Mark introduces John the Baptist, then Jesus, *then* Peter. Peter is a fisherman; he works with his little brother, Andrew, and they fish the Sea of Galilee. I get the impression it might be kind of difficult to be Peter's little brother, like he would have had a lot of opinions and advice about fishing, and well, probably about everything. But Peter is likely a lot of fun to be around. He's passionate, big, gregarious, interesting, and Jesus seems to really like him. Nearly the first thing Jesus does is to call Peter to follow him. In rapid succession, Jesus is baptized, duels with Satan, announces the beginning of his ministry, and then sees Peter. It is like he is rushing through this other stuff to get to Peter. Like he is walking fast, talking while he is walking, and then he sees Peter. Peter and his little brother are casting their nets into the sea. Jesus stops and immediately calls to them, tells them to follow him. Peter puts down his net and follows. Andrew follows his big brother.

The first person Jesus heals is Peter's mother-in-law. Jesus has picked up some other followers, John and his brother, James, but where do they all go for lunch, to hang out? Peter's house.

26

After traveling around a little and preaching and proclaiming and picking up more followers, Jesus decides to choose some people to be his inner circle, his closest students, his disciples. The first person he chooses is Peter. He not only chooses Peter first, but also bestows upon him a special name. Previously known as Simon, Jesus dubs him *Peter,* which—we all know from Sunday school—means "rock". Peter, like a rock, solid. By the end of the Gospel, I wonder if Jesus was not having a little good-natured fun with his pal, like nicknaming a big guy Tiny. Peter is the only disciple Jesus gives a nickname to. Well, he does dub James and John *Boanerges,* which Mark says means "Sons of Thunder," but that name doesn't really stick like the name *Peter* does. No one ever has to remind people in a Bible study that Boanerges used to be called James and John. There is no Epistle of Boanerges. Besides, the note in my revised *HarperCollins Study Bible* says, "Despite Mark's translation, both the derivation and meaning of *Boanerges* remains obscure" (Mark 3:17, note). It's not even a real name; Jesus probably made it up.

Peter displays both sides of his personality, his passion and his propensity to hypocrisy, when Jesus asks his disciples, "But who do you say that I am?" Peter answers without hesitation, "You are the Messiah" (Mark 8:29). He speaks right up. Then Jesus tells them all that he is going to be killed and after three days rise again. What? Peter doesn't like the sound of that, so he takes Jesus aside and rebukes him. He rebukes the man he has just declared the Messiah. He is likely telling him, "Look, Jesus, this is not a good plan. You can't be talking like this. We are trying to get something started here. So you can't be telling people you're going to be hated and murdered. It kind of kills the momentum, if you know what I mean." Peter, who claims to be a follower of the Messiah, can't seem to stop himself from trying to lead.

Jesus' response? Jesus rebukes *him.* He says, "Get behind me, Satan! For you are setting your mind not on divine things but on human things" (Mark 8:33). Jesus is saying, "You are in my way;

> Is Peter's declaration that Jesus is the Messiah "fake"? Does Peter truly understand who the Messiah is meant to be? As a Jew, what has he learned about who the Messiah is? Does he really mean it with all the passion he seems to have? Why would he then immediately try to take control of Jesus' actions? Is he aware of the contradiction of his own actions?

you are the devil." What kind of hypocrite declares Jesus the Messiah and then turns around and rebukes him? I would think that would sort of be the end of Peter's disciple career, but not at all. Peter continues to be Jesus' closest disciple. They seem to really like each other. Jesus knows what Peter is like and seems to be able to give as good as he gets from Peter.

To See Oneself Honestly

Hypocrisy is an old word, which is a good thing, because it has a history that is rich and full. Using my sophisticated research tools (i.e., looking up the word on Wikipedia—note: If you try this, be sure to read the article about the word *hypocrisy* and not the one about the heavy metal band *Hypocrisy*!), I learned that the ancient Greek word it is based on means "to play a part." *Hypocrite* was the word used for an actor. The term got its negative spin when, in fourth-century Athens, one senator ridiculed another who had been an actor before taking up politics, saying that, because he was a hypocrite (an actor), nothing he said could be taken as authentic. The former actor was so skilled at playing a part, his oration could not be trusted. I guess authenticity was big even six thousand years ago.

The word has another shade to it as well. It can be "understood as an amalgam of the Greek prefix *hypo*, meaning 'under,' and the verb *krinier*, meaning 'to sift or decide.' Thus the original meaning is given as a deficiency in the ability to sift or decide. This deficiency, as it pertains to one's own beliefs and feelings, does well to inform the word's contemporary meaning" (Online Etymology Dictionary). Hypocrisy is the inability to evaluate oneself accurately, to see oneself honestly.

This idea is also found in psychology. The *fundamental attribution error,* first posed by Fritz Heider in his 1958 book, *The Psychology of Interpersonal Relations,* is a concept that says that people are more likely to explain actions of their own that contradict a held belief by pointing to circumstances. But when they see the same hypocrisy in others, they attribute it to a character defect.

When I see someone else saying one thing and doing the opposite, it is clear to me that the person is a hypocrite—a phony or a fake. When I say one thing and do the opposite, however, there is a perfectly good explanation; you know, everyone makes mistakes. Being fake is a charge leveled by one person against another. Very rarely do we set out to act hypocritically—to act fake or phony on purpose. We might not always reveal our true selves; we might choose to disguise or obscure less desirable qualities—but we wouldn't call ourselves phonies (even when we Photoshop our profile pictures on Facebook or eHarmony). In many cases, we are unable to evaluate ourselves accurately. Most people, like the apostle Paul, do things we don't want to do and don't do things we desire to do. And the real kicker is that, a lot of the time, we are not aware that we are acting hypocritically. Hopefully, we have someone around to point it out, and when they do, we have the grace not to react defensively but confessionally.

So a helpful way to look at hypocrisy is not to think about the way I appear to others, but to think about my ability to evaluate myself accurately. I should be concerned with telling myself the truth about who I am and what kinds of deception or misdeeds I am capable of. I should be able to admit that I do not always live out what I believe, that sometimes I do things that contradict my core values, that I may even represent myself in ways that are not true. And when I do these things, I should freely admit them and ask for forgiveness and seek reconciliation.

> **Are most people, Christian or non-Christian, aware when they are acting hypocritically? Are most hypocrites purposeful or accidental hypocrites? Are you? Why?**

Things between Jesus and Peter appear to be patched up pretty quickly. Jesus takes Peter, James, and John up to the top of a mountain with him. There Jesus begins to glow, Moses and Elijah appear, and the three of them begin talking. What is Peter's reaction to seeing Jesus transfigured and having a conversation with the father of the Torah and the chief of all the Prophets? Does he fall on his knees and worship? Stand in stunned silence and reverence? No, he interrupts the conversation—he butts in. He tries to take charge again. He says to Jesus, Moses, and Elijah, "Okay, guys, here is what we need to do: we should build three altars, one for each of you." This time Jesus doesn't rebuke him. It has gone too far for that. God the Father has to speak to Peter this time. A voice comes out of the clouds telling Peter, "This is my Son; listen to him! Peter, Jesus is the Messiah here. You listen to him. He's in charge—get it?" (Mark 9:2-8).

A little later, Peter is perplexed—I might even say hurt—when Jesus tells the disciples about how hard it is for anyone to enter the kingdom of God. Peter evidently thought he already had a place reserved, that he deserved it. He says to Jesus, "Look, we have left everything and followed you; that's not enough?" (Mark 10:28).

Authenticity and You

Because both Christians and non-Christians in these postmodern generations are so acutely aware of issues of authenticity, they know how hard it is to find and to live out genuineness. At House of Mercy, we've always been very sensitive to the issue of authenticity. From the beginning, one of our mantras was "Tell the truth." You might think that this would be assumed when you start a church, but what we meant by "Tell the truth" was be real, be authentic in everything we do, from what our bulletin covers look like to the message on the answering machine to the coffee we serve to the way we read and talk about the Bible. We felt that if we used a bulletin cover that we had ordered from some church supply company or had grabbed an image from a clip-art program, people would walk in the church and look at that and think, "What is this? What does this have to do with anything? This is just another generic product. Is that what I can expect from this church?" Instead, we have different people from the community design our covers. The covers range from a cut-and-paste punk rock collage, made with headlines ripped from the newspaper and kitschy drawings from thirty-year-old Sunday school material, to slick, professionally designed juxtapositions of cultural objects, to a simple drawing of our church building placed upside down.

When you call the House of Mercy and get the machine, you don't get a message dripping with pseudo-sincerity, selling our welcoming attitude or trying to impress upon you what a successful, full-service church we are. No, we tell you where we are and what time we worship, and we close by saying, "You should come. It's not that bad."

Now the place where authenticity, being real, and truth-telling matter the most is in interpreting the Bible. This is where you have to tell the truth, and maybe sometimes it's the hardest thing to do.

Preaching begins with reading and asking questions. Asking real questions, authentic, honest questions. Questions you don't already know the answers to. If you already know the answers, they are not real questions. If you bring these fake questions into your sermon, you are just preaching the absorbed reading of the text. The congregation already knows the answers, too. This then is not a sermon; it is a consensus. At best, it is patting each other on the back; at worst it is very boring. A real question is not an agreement; it is an invitation. It is engaging. The people may be confused, but they will not be bored.

Some verses seem to make no sense, or they seem to contain no hint of the Good News. If you find the right questions, you will find the Good News. If a verse scares you or bugs you or dumb-founds you, then that is a real question. If you have to think about a verse for more than twenty minutes, then that is a real question. If a verse makes you fall in love, believe in God, feel giddy, then that is a real question.

If, by the time we are, say, twenty years old, or thirty or fifty or a hundred, we could answer all the questions raised in the Holy Scriptures about the one true God of mercy who allowed his creation to kill him and then made that very murder the means of the salvation of the world—maybe we have the wrong questions.

Or at least not enough questions. The God of our faith is expansive, mysterious, sometimes confounding, beyond our complete understanding, but also inviting. The God of our faith invites us into real conversations that include deep and difficult questions. Are there ways we could bring that kind of conversation and biblical interpretation, including our very real questions, into the sermon? When we do, we produce a proclamation that resonates with the new generations. While it is hard to convince postmoderns that one group or expression of faith has the right answers, they (like Peter) are ready to engage with people (like Jesus) who are asking real and complex questions.

For most of my life, I was taught, though not explicitly, that the kind of real, deep, challenging questions about God, Jesus, the Holy Spirit, the Bible, creation, miracles, etc. were not so much questions but really confessions of my lack of faith. If that is the underlying message of a preacher to the congregation, it is going to be really hard to bring those kinds of questions or confessions into a sermon. But confessing to a lack of faith sometimes can be the Good News, because it is honest, and it is a feeling that many people can identify with. And then the emphasis is not on the strength of my faith in God, but on the strength of God's love and faith in me. Acknowledging my own hypocrisy as an inevitable and even essential part of my humanity liberates me to experience God's strength more fully.

Let's go back to Peter. The incident that really earns him the title of Big-Time Hypocrite happens the night of Jesus' arrest. The disciples are all sitting around the table sharing the Passover meal, and Jesus tells them that he is going to give his life for them and that this is the last meal they will have together until they enter the kingdom of God. And finally, on the Mount of Olives, Jesus mentions one last thing: The disciples all are going to desert him. Peter speaks up right away, as is his habit, and straightens Jesus out. He says maybe everyone else will desert Jesus, but not him. He would never, could never. Jesus tells him that, as a matter of fact, he will, this very night, deny him three times. Peter is exasperated and offended. Mark writes that Peter "vehemently" says, "Even though I must die with you, I will not deny you" (Mark 14:31).

Well, we know how the story ends, but even before Peter gets a chance to prove Jesus right, he has a whole night to display his hypocrisy. Jesus takes Peter, James, and John to pray with him at Gethsemane. He tells them he is "deeply grieved, even to death" (Mark 14:34). So he asks them to sit with him while he prays, to stay awake with him. Of course, they fall asleep. Jesus wakes them up and asks, "Simon, are you asleep?" (Mark 14:37). He must be really upset to go back to calling him Simon. He tells them again, "Keep awake," and they fall asleep. This happens three times. A few hours earlier, Peter had said that he would die rather than betray Jesus, but now he can't even stay awake and pray for him when Jesus needs him.

The priests come with a crowd to arrest Jesus; Peter and all the disciples run off and desert him. Peter sneaks back. He follows Jesus and his captors at a distance, hiding, not wanting to be seen, but he is spotted by a woman who says, "Hey, you were with that Jesus troublemaker!" And Peter denies it, denies it, denies it. What happened to "Everyone else may deny you, but I would die first"? The hypocrite. Just like you. Just like me. Jesus knows it better than anyone—and loves us all the same.

> Jesus knows something about who Peter is, but Peter denies this truth. What would our lives look like if we could rely on others to help us see our shortcomings? What if we reacted confessionally and not defensively?

Telling the Truth about Tensions

When House of Mercy started in the mid-'90s, the televangelist scandals were still fresh in people's minds, and the prosperity gospel was making the news. These young, cynical people who were coming to our church, many of them from outside any church experience, were very skeptical about churches asking for money. We were aware of this, so at first we didn't ask for money; we had no liturgy of giving or offering during the worship service. And guess what? We didn't get any money. Even the pastors were uncomfortable with asking for money, especially since the majority of that money went to pay our salaries. We quickly realized that, to keep the doors open, we would have to talk about money in some way. We didn't think it was completely honest to say, "When you give your money to House of Mercy, you are giving it to God." What would God do with money? That was not true. People would be giving it to an organization that used it to pay salaries and bills. But we didn't want to say that the money would only be used for salaries and bills. We felt that giving monetary gifts to the church was a way of acknowledging that we can give because we have first received the possibility of all things from God. We believed that giving away some of our money was a way to acknowledge that we strive to be free of the economic system that runs the world, not exchanging value for value but living out the upside-down values of the kingdom of God. So we came up with a statement that we felt told the truth about both of those realities.

We also understand that people are in different places on their faith journeys. Some people just come to the church because they find it interesting, and they don't have a Christian commitment.

Others have a commitment that is profound and have a spiritual practice of giving that is rooted in responding to the grace of God. But for most people, there is a tension, and so we sought to acknowledge that in the statement. We came up with the following:

> We acknowledge (confess) the dialectical nature of an invitation to give away your money. We believe that giving away our money is a way to act outside the economy, outside the system that runs the world. It frees us and allows us to act out the truth that we can give because we have first received all things from God—it is an act of worship. On the other hand, we are asking you to give away your money to the House of Mercy, an institution (however well purposed) that very much needs your money to exist. So, an invitation to give away your money, to free yourself and to acknowledge God's gifts could seem a little, what? Self-interested? We want to assure you, we understand this dialectic, and we want to affirm both the freedom in this act of worship and the self-interested appeal for financial support.
>
> Whether you give as an act of freedom and worship or only because you want to support what House of Mercy is doing—or an unresolved mixture of both—we are very grateful.

The truth is that a lot of what we do as a church and as individuals is motivated by an unresolved mixture of both self-interest and the desire to live out our faith. Does this make us hypocrites? The hypocrisy comes when we do not tell the truth about the tensions, to ourselves first and to others. Could it be that even our motivation to understand and reach the new generations is an example of this unresolved mixture? I have been in a few board meetings at House of Mercy where conversations about budget shortfalls quickly turned into conversations about evangelism and outreach—

how we can get more people to come to church. The shame is not in admitting that we want more people to come to church and to bring their money with them—that is what everyone is thinking. The shame comes in pretending that our motivation for a particular outreach event or evangelistic program is purely to share the mercy of Jesus with people. It is okay to admit that we *wish* our motivations were purely to share the mercy of Jesus with people, but that we can't help thinking that more people at church could help us with our budget shortfall. It is the truth.

Can we avoid being hypocrites? Can we practice what we preach? If we preach the Good News of Jesus Christ—the unconditional love and sacrifice of a Creator for his creation that leads to reconciliation for the world, and that God calls us to live out that unconditional love—then it is impossible to practice what we preach. By no means should we preach something different; instead, we should understand perfection to be beyond us. Any success at loving God and neighbor only occurs when Christ is acting in us.

Postmodern generations understand the inability to completely become the person one desires to be. No one has a completely accurate and honest understanding of who he or she is. Peter surely did not. Peter was such a great hypocrite because he did not have an accurate understanding of his own fear or his inability to let someone else (even the Messiah) be in control. He wasn't realistic about both sides of his nature. Peter was a hypocrite; I am a hypocrite; people who say that Christians are hypocrites are hypocrites; and you are probably a hypocrite. It is part of who we are as humans. That fact did not rule out Peter as Jesus' trusted friend and disciple. When the women find the empty tomb at the end of Mark's Gospel, a man there has a message for them: "Go, tell his disciples and Peter that he is going ahead of you to Galilee" (Mark 16:7). Peter is one of the first people Jesus wants to see after his defeat of death.

■ nuChristians seek an accurate and honest understanding of who they are.

■ nuChristians are DIYers (do it yourselfers); they don't repackage and try to sell an old product.

■ nuChristians are honest about contradictions, tensions, and ambiguities.

■ nuChristians seek authenticity in their relationships and in their faith.

■ nuChristians trust the transforming love of Jesus over their personal ability to be perfect.

CHAPTER 4

The Reconciling Love of God

*"Now I know that there is no God in all
the earth except in Israel"*
(2 Kings 5:15).

Do You Want to Get Saved?

I come from born-again people. I have done my time on street corners on two continents, asking perfect strangers if they knew where they would spend eternity if they died that day. "Go to hell," was sometimes the response I got. Other times, and more rarely, someone would answer the question in an open-ended way that allowed me to go through my whole routine, which would end with the question, "Would you like to pray with me, right now, and accept Jesus as your personal Lord and Savior?" Mostly, though, people were polite but dismissive. In all my street-corner witnessing, friendship evangelism, lifestyle evangelism, and conversational/apologetic efforts, I think I only prayed the sinner's prayer with two people. And one of them, I'm sure, was pretending because he felt sorry and embarrassed for me.

When I remember kneeling on the sidewalk at the corner of Lexington and Summit with Mike Ackerman, lining out a prayer for him to repeat after me, eyes clamped shut but sneaking peeks from time to time, only to catch Mike Ackerman sneaking peeks back at me, I still feel embarrassed—but also a little sympathetic for my younger self. I was just doing what I was taught to do. I was doing what I thought was required of me. I was doing what I believed to be the most important thing anyone could do. I was helping to save his teenage soul from hell.

Mike Ackerman died three years later of a new, and at the time, untreatable disease that some would say was a result of his unchristian lifestyle. I met with Mike quite a few times in the last year of his life. He came to me asking the big questions and talking about his fear, about all he would miss in life, and about all the people whom he loved and had hurt. I responded by reminding him of that afternoon on Lexington and Summit, when he had committed his life to Christ. I begged him to repent, both assuring him of his salvation and pleading with him to recommit his life to Jesus. He eventually got frustrated and stopped calling me. At the time, I wondered if I was helping him at all. In retrospect, it's clear to me that I was not.

Is there a perception among non-Christians that evangelicals are only interested in saving souls? Is that perception true? When I was a young evangelical, saving souls was very important to me for this simple reason: if someone had not accepted Jesus Christ as his or her personal Lord and Savior, that person would spend eternity in hell. Every time I failed to take advantage of an opportunity to witness to somebody, that person's eternal damnation was on my head. Even at the time, however, I was also motivated by something else. I really did believe, as I still do, that the love and mercy of Jesus would set people free and give them abundant life.

What does it mean to get saved, to be saved? What do we need to be saved from? Is it hell and eternal damnation? Is it from ourselves? Is it from the kingdom of the world and the life that barely resembles the abundant possibility of true life in Christ? Maybe salvation looks different from the way we always thought it did.

Compelled by Love

The story of Naaman, found in 2 Kings 5, is a salvation story. Not a salvation story in the way we traditionally think of it, but a story of an individual being transformed by the action of God's mercy in his life.

> **What motivates the servant girl to suggest that Naaman go to the prophet of Israel? If this is the first step to Naaman's salvation and transformation, how can this example serve as a model for us?**

Naaman was the commander of the Syrian army in the time when Benhadad II ruled Aram (Syria) and Jehoram was the king of Israel. He was a friend and trusted adviser to his king. While his name and his deeds where known throughout the country, only those closest to him knew that Naaman suffered from leprosy, a skin disease. At the time, diseases of the skin were thought to be a punishment for the sin of slander, gossip, or deception. So it really didn't look very good for a close adviser to the king to have that particular disease.

His condition was kept quiet. But a servant in Naaman's household, a young girl who had been captured from Israel in a raid, noticed Naaman's disease. She told his wife that if he went to the great prophet of Israel, he would be healed. Naaman went to his king and told him what the servant girl had said. The king said to him, "Go then, and I will send along a letter to the king of Israel."

Love People; Don't Save Them

We are not called to save people; we are called to love people. You don't love people by trying to sell them something or convince them of something. Jesus loved people by being in relationship with them, knowing them, engaging them, healing them. Love does not have an ulterior motive. That's why friendship evangelism is a lie. You're not really being somebody's friend if your purpose for befriending them is to get them to do something you want them to do. That's called manipulation.

Another insidious nugget in the witnessing/soul-saving canon is the idea of lifestyle evangelism. That's where you live a life of perfection and righteousness, exuding love and practicing acts of charity, so others will observe you and ask, "How is it that you have come to be thus? And what must I do to have such a life?" This lie is more destructive to the witness than to the "witnessee", because it perpetuates the notion that an individual can live a life of perfection, and that it is the perfection of the individual witness life that is the act that leads to reconciliation. It can only be and always is the movement of God leads to reconciliation.

People need to be saved, reconciled, and transformed, but that is not our calling. Can we put an injunction on saving people? Saving someone's soul cannot be the motivation for engaging them. Love people, enjoy people, serve people, be a part of their lives, but leave saving their souls alone—that's God's business, the work of the Holy Spirit. That might sound crazy and radical. What about the Great Commission? What about hell?

The Great Commission, referring to Matthew 28:19-20, says, "Go therefore and make disciples of all nations, baptizing them in the name of the Father and of the Son and of the Holy Spirit, and teaching them to obey everything that I have commanded you. And remember, I am with you always to the end of the age." Making disciples sounds a lot more like the process of loving people, serving people, being with people, and teaching them about the kingdom of God than it does getting someone to make a verbal commitment to a mitigation deal regarding the eternal state of his or her soul.

And what about hell? I really think the doctrine of hell, damnation, and eternal suffering has led to the greatest of all perversions of what it means to be a Christian. It twists the Good News of the gospel of the kingdom of God to the point where it resembles the systems that run our world. What I mean by that is that it takes Jesus' message of love and mercy and modifies it. Hell gives Christianity a product to sell. *Fire insurance* it has been called in more than one kitschy, old-time tract. That old-style, street-corner, door-to-door witnessing is rarely practiced by anyone but the most fundamentalist of believers today. But it is interesting to me to think about the way that old method of selling the fire insurance product reflected the sales practices of its day. In an era where there were no shopping malls, and door-to-door salesmen were common, Christian fire insurance salesmen simply used the same methods prevalent in the culture at the time.

But that was a long time ago. Imagine if somebody came to your house today with a suitcase full of samples and asked if he could come in and sit down and show you his products. I don't know many people who would let him in. I think most people would think he is a scam artist or some kind of criminal. So it's not surprising that the door-to-door, street-corner method of selling the "Jesus product" is no longer widely used. (Besides, now we do have shopping malls and sophisticated marketing and subtler techniques of selling things.)

The sophistication and the subtlety are reflected in the fact that not too many Christians or churches really talk about hell much anymore. A lot of evangelical Christians are still out there trying to save souls, but they are selling the Christian product with a more positive spin on it. But at the heart of it, I still think a large part of the motivation is keeping people out of hell.

People need to be reconciled to God through Christ. And the Good News of the Gospels, of the whole New Testament, is that God is in Christ reconciling the world. Another way to talk about it is transformation. People need to be transformed. We live in a world that historically and culturally has been dominated by a system that is antithetical to the kingdom of God.

It is a system that postmodern generations struggle with. They understand that, like all of us, they are entrenched in it, but at the same time they are very critical of it. It is a system that values power above all else: financial power, physical power, personal power. The new generations value community and the flattening of hierarchies. They value an equal distribution of power in organizations, and they value conversations over regulations. The cornerstone of the kingdom of God is Jesus, willingly giving up his power and dying. Giving up power is an act of love, and love is the rule of the kingdom of God. We are not called to *save* people; we are called to *love* people. Jesus says, in John, "I give you a new commandment, that you love one another. Just as I have loved you, you also should love one another. By this everyone will know you are my disciples, if you have love for one another" (John 13:34-35). He says the same thing in Matthew, Mark, and Luke, with some slight variations. Jesus replied: "'Love the Lord your God with all your heart and with all your soul and with all your mind.' This is the first and greatest commandment. And the second is like it: 'Love your neighbor as yourself.' All the Law and the Prophets hang on these two commandments" (Matthew 22:37-40; Mark 12:30-31; Luke 10:27 TNIV).

The Making of a Disciple

Naaman took the letter his king had given him and went to the king of Israel. Naaman presented the letter to the king, and Jehoram unsealed it and read, "When this letter reaches you, know that I have sent you my servant Naaman, that you may cure him of his leprosy." The king Jehoram tore his clothes and said, "Am I God, to give death or life, that this man sends word to me to cure a man of his leprosy? Just look and see how he is trying to pick a quarrel with me" (2 Kings 5:6-7).

The prophet the young girl spoke of, Elisha, heard about the situation and told the king to send Naaman to him. Naaman pulled up in front of Elisha's house with his chariots, horses, and the kind of entourage that said he was someone very important. Elisha sent a servant out to him with a message, "Go, wash in the Jordan seven times, and your flesh shall be restored and you shall be clean" (2 Kings 5:10).

Naaman was offended. He had expected a bit more ceremony, at the very least that the prophet would have come out and talked to him. The prophet sent a messenger? Naaman knew how these things were supposed to be done. There should be some sacrifices, some fire, a few rituals, some calling out to the gods. This was insulting. Naaman got mad and told his servants, in so many words, "Who does he think he is? I come all this way, and he sends someone to tell me to go wash in the Jordan? I could have washed in any river in Syria, and it would be better than this. Mount up everyone; we are going home." But one of his servants came to him and said, "Look, if the prophet had told you to do something really complicated or hard in order to heal you, you would have done it, so why won't you do something easy?"

Naaman reluctantly went down to the river and washed in it seven times, and on the seventh time, when he came out, his skin was smooth like that of a young boy. He had been completely healed. It was only then that Naaman realized that he had never actually thought it possible, that he had thought that he would never be completely healed. And now he had the realization that he no longer had to hide his skin, to cover up, to live in the fear of being suspected of deception or some other dark sin. It was as if he were breathing fully for the first time. Naaman stood up straighter and taller than he felt he ever had, and he took a deep breath, filling his lungs with oxygen and feeling a kind of new life coursing through his body. He felt free. He and all his party left immediately to return to Elisha's house. This time they were brought inside, and they stood before the prophet.

Naaman proclaimed, "Now I know that there is no God in all the earth except in Israel" (2 Kings 5:15). He presented gifts of silver and gold and fine cloth to Elisha, but Elisha would not accept them. Naaman pleaded with him to take something for healing him. Elisha still refused, saying that it was the God he served who had healed him. Then Naaman said, "If not, please let two mule-loads of earth be given to your servants; for your servant will no longer offer burnt offering or sacrifice to any god except the LORD. But may the LORD pardon your servant on one count: when my master goes into the house of Rimmon to worship there, leaning on my arm, and I blow down in the house of Rimmon, when I do bow down in the house of Rimmon, may the LORD pardon your servant on this one count." (2 Kings 5:17-18)

Elisha looked at Naaman and said, "Go in peace."

A Salvation Story?

This is a remarkable story. Naaman is saved. He is healed, relieved of his sin. He proclaims that there is no other god but the God of Israel and that he will never bow down to any other god but the one true God. All that is great; let us all rejoice—except there is one more thing. He actually will be going back to his country, an enemy of Israel, and he will be bowing down regularly to another god, but he says he will not really mean it. Naaman will pretend it is the God of Israel. And he has the nerve to ask Elisha, "Do you think that will be all right?" And Elisha says, "Yes, go in peace. Yeah, that will be okay."

What a beautiful irony that a man with leprosy, a disease believed to be the result of the sin of deception, is healed, and now that man is given permission by the prophet of God to be deceptive in his worship, to lie about who he believes God truly is.

The fact that he asks permission to accompany his king to the temple of Rimmon to worship makes it clear that he is going to return to his country, return to his position as the leader of Ben-hadad II's armies. I can only assume that when there are further skirmishes between Israel and Syria that Naaman is there leading the charge.

How will anyone know that Naaman has been saved by God if he pretends to worship the false god of Syria? What about Naaman's witness? Salvation, it seems, looks different than we expect sometimes.

This is the kind of salvation story that is practically beyond our understanding. It defies the boundaries of our understanding of

> **Does knowing if someone is saved or not change the way we treat them? Would we reach out to the new generations to love them as our neighbor even if we knew there was no chance that they would ever attend our church?**

what a salvation scenario is supposed to look like. I like this story because it starts with a young girl who sees the suffering of another and points him in the direction of the God of mercy, the God of Israel. She doesn't think about the fact that Naaman is the general of her country's enemy. She doesn't like the fact that Naaman's armies have captured her and have taken her from her home to serve as a slave in Naaman's house. She is not worried that the God of Israel will strike Naaman down for worshiping a false god and waging war on God's people. She is moved by compassion and motivated by a basic love for her fellow human, for her neighbor. She believes in a God of love and mercy that would heal Naaman.

God loves Naaman. In spite of who he is or what he does, God recognizes Naaman's worship, even if it is hidden or unconventional. God is not interested in the regulations of salvation. God is interested in the restoration of relationships with all of God's children. So many of those restored relationships, those salvation stories, look different than we might expect. We might not even recognize them at all.

Trust the Holy Spirit

Relationship is also one of the highest values for these new generations. They often talk about their tribes, meaning the group of people whom they trust, share things in common with, and care about. Postmoderns are much more likely to try a new church experience if a member of their tribe invites them than they are if they see an advertisement or have a onetime encounter with a stranger.

When we first started House of Mercy, we knew that people might be showing up who had experienced the door-to-door, fire insurance sales pitch in the past. And that they might be a little bit leery about coming to a church, even if someone they trusted had told them about it. We kept the lights really low in the back half of the church so people would feel comfortable sneaking out in the middle of the service if they wanted to. We held to the old Alcoholics Anonymous adage that people should come as the result of attraction, not promotion. Never at any point in the service do we tell people they need to be saved or that they should be Christians. We just try to preach the gospel and interpret the Scriptures in a way that points to Jesus, to be clear about what we believe, as well as to be clear about our struggles to believe. The only invitation to take any kind of action is when we come to the communion table at the end of every service. We stand behind the table, with the bread and the cup in front of us, spread our arms wide, and say, "This is the Lord's table, and *all* are welcome."

We don't keep track of who identifies himself as a Christian and who identifies himself as a non-Christian, or an atheist, or a semi-Buddhist, or whatever. We believe that the body and the blood of Christ were given for all, for the forgiveness of the sins of all. We believe it's the job of the Holy Spirit to move people, transform them, and compel them to come forward and share in Christ's redemptive meal. Recently a young musician who has been coming to the church for about five years came forward and took communion for the first time. I couldn't help noticing, but I did not want to say anything to him, so I just smiled a little. At the end of the service, he kind of bounded up to me. With a huge grin on his face, he said, "That sermon, man. I got it. Not just the sermon, the whole thing!" I smiled a lot then. He must have heard a couple hundred sermons, played music at the church countless times, and spent countless hours hanging out with the House of Mercy tribe. Then on that particular Sunday, he realized something had been happening to him. And he responded, eagerly, excitedly, joyfully. Like someone who had fallen in love.

On first meeting someone new, most people don't sit down and make a commitment to be in an intimate relationship with that person. We get to know someone over time. We find out more about the person, and the way we feel about them grows. We start to live life together. This is how people come to know Jesus; this is how we are called to make disciples.

- nuChristians are compelled by love to form relationships.
- nuChristians see reconciliation with God through Christ as the work of the Holy Spirit.
- nuChristians make disciples, not converts.
- nuChristians welcome everyone into the body of Christ.
- nuChristians are grateful for the transforming love of God.

CHAPTER 5

Judged with God's Mercy

"All who have sinned apart from the law will also perish apart from the law, and all who have sinned under the law will be judged by the law"
(Romans 2:12).

Without Judgment

The new generations are natives of a world where homogeneity is a nearly a thing of the past. Technology and globalization have transformed our culture in ways that expose us to people, ideas, religions, and lifestyles that are vastly different from our own. For many in the Baby Boomer generation, those kinds of differences are seen as undesirable, intrusive, threatening, even wrong. For postmoderns, living with people who have different ideas, religions, and lifestyles is assumed. The culture they live in has been that way all their lives. It might be hard for them to imagine a culture were everyone looks the same, thinks the same, lives the same way, and believes the same things. So, for example, when they hear the harsh judgment of homosexuals coming from some sectors of evangelical Christianity, they may dismiss all Christians as ignorant and intolerant.

> What, if anything, in our hyperdiverse, multicultural, multilifestyle society should we be judging? To what extent, if at all, are we required to try to change the offending person?

Divorcing Judgment from Your Faith

When I was a young evangelical, it seemed like the worst thing anyone could possibly do was to get a divorce. Divorce was scandalous and worldly. I had been taught that it was an undeniable truth that once two people were married, no matter what happened, God wanted them to stay married. I remember when Jenny and Cindy Ferguson's mom and dad got a divorce. I was eight, and it scared me. They lived across the street from us, and their mom would watch my siblings and me sometimes after school. Their dad was never around that much; he must have been at work, but I was never really sure what he did. They seemed normal, but I do remember Mrs. Ferguson once asking me what I thought about "women's lib," as it was called back then. I didn't really know what to say. I just remember having this weird kind of feeling, like, that's not something you're supposed to be talking to a kid about. Other than that and the fact that they were Lutheran (which was only slightly more Christian than atheists and Catholics), they seemed like regular, good people.

When they got divorced, nobody really said anything about it. One day Mr. Ferguson was just not there. My dad did sit us kids down and tell us, but that was it. I never saw Mr. Ferguson again. Mrs. Ferguson got a real estate license, and shortly after that, they moved away. I think what scared me about Jenny and Cindy Ferguson's mom and dad getting a divorce was how shrouded it all seemed to me as a kid. I had been taught that divorce was bad. And I believed you were bad if you got a divorce, and there were certain kinds of people who got divorced—bad people—people who weren't Christians or were bad Christians. It didn't really *seem* like Mr. and Mrs. Ferguson were bad, but I thought they had to be, and somehow I applied that badness to Jenny and Cindy. And, as if to confirm how evil divorce was, divorce had made them disappear. My brother Mike and I played with Jenny and Cindy every day after school and after dinner, but then one day, in came divorce,

> **How have your judgments about divorce (or other controversial topics) changed over the years? To what extent are changes in your personal judgments reflected in society or the church? Why?**

and three weeks later they vanished. We never saw Jenny and Cindy again. It was as if divorce was so bad, it had swallowed them all up in its darkness.

The Judgment of the Righteous

Saul of Tarsus enters the biblical narrative in a dramatic and nefarious scene. There is no mention of him before he is found at the scene of the stoning of Stephen. Luke paints the scene masterfully in only a few words. An enraged crowd surges forward and seizes Stephen, dragging him to the outskirts of town. Stephen doesn't struggle but looks beyond them. His calm in the midst of this chaos is mirrored by only one man, who walks calmly but determinedly at the rear of the crowd. When the crowd is outside the gates of the city, before they take up rocks to pummel Stephen to death, they take off their coats and place them at the feet of the stoic young man with piercing eyes: Saul. Luke concludes the scene of Stephen's death with the stark words, "And Saul approved of their killing him" (Acts 8:1).

Saul goes on to lead the persecution of the Christians. He goes from house to house, dragging men and women out and throwing them in prison. Luke says, "Saul was ravaging the church" (Acts 8:3). The scene conjures up images of soldiers going door to door, searching for insurgents. Up until then, Christians had been seen as another sect of Judaism, with the right to enter and speak in the synagogues, and had experienced very little persecution. Saul ratcheted the situation up to the next level and sought to carry his crusade beyond Jerusalem. He went to the high priest and asked for letters to bring to the synagogue in Damascus, giving him permission to seek out Christians and bring them, bound, back to

Jerusalem for punishment. And off he went, "breathing threats and murder" (Acts 9:1-2), confident in his righteous judgment of the Christian minority.

One Flesh

When I was in tenth grade and a member of Teen Missions International, we had to memorize Bible verses, a lot of Bible verses. And one of the passages was Matthew 19:3-12, Jesus' teaching about divorce. In it, the Pharisees come to Jesus to test him and ask him, "Is it lawful for a man to divorce his wife for any cause?" Jesus answers:

> "Have you not read that the one who made them at the beginning 'made them male and female,' and said, 'For this reason a man shall leave his father and mother and be joined to his wife, and the two shall become one flesh'?…what God has joined together, let no one separate." They said to him, "Why then did Moses command us to give a certificate of dismissal and to divorce her?" He said to them, "It was because you were so hard-hearted that Moses allowed you to divorce your wives, but from the beginning it was not so. And I say to you, whoever divorces his wife, except for unchastity, and marries another commits adultery."

There it is, right there in the Bible. Divorce is sin. I had it memorized (although I memorized it in the King James Version). This verse was also used to warn us about premarital sex. Like, if you ever join together with someone else, you become one flesh, so you're married. Then if you marry someone else and have sex with them, you're committing adultery. Even as a kid, something about this interpretation seemed a little off. But that's another discussion.

When I read those verses now, I see something else going on. Why did the Pharisees ask him this question? The text says they asked him to test him. They asked Jesus, "Is it lawful for a man to divorce his wife for any reason?" It seems to me, by virtue of the fact that it was the Pharisees who asked him this particular question, that the subject was up for debate, that different rabbis might have had differing opinions on the topic. It was a debate about the interpretation of Scripture, of the few particular passages dealing with divorce. That was what the Pharisees were referring to when they said, "Why then did Moses command us to give a certificate of dismissal and to divorce her?" Because the common understanding was that Moses wrote the Law, the Pentateuch, the Scripture.

One possible set of verses the Pharisees might have been referring to is Deuteronomy 24:1-4, which says:

> Suppose a man enters into marriage with a woman, but she does not please him because he finds something objectionable about her, and so he writes her a certificate of divorce, puts it in her hand, and sends her out of his house; she then leaves his house and goes off to become another man's wife. And suppose the second man dislikes her, writes her a bill of divorce, puts it in her hand, and sends her out of his house (or the second man who marries her dies); her first husband, who sent her away, is not permitted to take her again to be his wife after she has been defiled; for that would be abhorrent to the LORD, and you shall not bring guilt on the land that the LORD your God is giving you as a possession.

Yes, possession is what it seems to be all about. The woman was the man's property, an asset, his to do with what he wanted. So if he didn't want her anymore for some reason, such as, maybe she was getting older and he wanted a young wife, or he married her because her father was rich and she came with a bunch of cattle but he never really liked her that much to begin with, no problem!

> **What effect does culture have on what we think are sins? How might our understanding of what is sin change?**

He could just grab a piece of paper and a pen, write out the divorce certificate, and send the woman from his home. If she was lucky, she might be able to return to her father or find another man to marry her. A woman alone in that culture was vulnerable, physically and economically; her options would have been limited—most likely to begging or harlotry.

If a woman, for some reason doesn't like her husband anymore (maybe he treats her like a piece of property, for instance) she has no options. If she meets someone else, someone she likes better, maybe someone younger or nicer, she only has one option: adultery.

So when Jesus, says, "What God has joined together let no one separate," perhaps he is not talking about divorce in the same way we understand it. He's changing the issue from one of property rights to a matter of human rights, to the rights of the woman. He is saying that a man doesn't have a right to put a woman on the street just because he feels like it. Even though the Scripture, God's law, written by Moses, gives the man that right, Jesus feels comfortable rejecting that approach, based on a higher commandment: the commandment to love one another.

Culture and Hot-Button Sin

What changed? How did what was once considered the gravest of sins and a threat to the bedrock of society come to be seen as an unfortunate but not uncommon part of life for many people? The Scriptures concerning divorce haven't changed. Jesus' words haven't changed, but many people's understanding of those words have. I would guess that even those who consider divorce a sin today would not judge it in the same way that they might have thirty years ago.

Maybe the fact that the Pharisees even asked Jesus the question about divorce suggests that some kind of cultural shift was occurring in first-century Palestine regarding the nature of marriage. They knew that there was a different interpretation of the Mosaic laws about divorce out there, and they wanted to see if Jesus came down on the right side of the issue.

Perhaps it was a cultural shift in the 1970s that led to divorce becoming a hot-button sin of the time. The Equal Rights Amendment was being voted on by the states and debated everywhere from capitals to carpools. The feminist movement was making its first cultural splash, and there was a fear that women would start walking away from their families in droves. There was some truth behind those fears. As women began to understand that they did have choices, that they could work outside the house, could have fulfilling careers, could support themselves, many more women chose to leave unfulfilling or destructive marriages. Divorce was being seen, increasingly, as an acceptable option, and this fact contributed to its elevation as one of the hot-button issues of the time.

Passing Judgment

The most recent hot-button sin is homosexuality. I think it is the increasing acceptance of gay and lesbian relationships that has brought the topic to the forefront of the culture wars, in the same way that the growing acceptance of divorce brought it to the forefront in the '70s and '80s. Recent laws passed in several states permitting same-sex marriage triggered an immediate response from conservative Christians all over the country. Laws to ban same-sex marriage were brought to state houses everywhere. Many of them passed.

I'm not going to enter the scriptural debate over whether there is a basis for calling same-sex relationships sin. I don't think they are sinful, but I know and respect people on both sides of the issue. I hope that my spiritual and cultural exploration of a previous hot button, divorce, as well as my reading of Saul's gross misjudgment based on his righteousness, understanding of Scripture, and passion, might be instructive in thinking about the issue of homosexuality.

The point is not to argue issue by issue that which should be considered sin and that which should be judged. It's the whole idea of judgment that needs to be reconsidered. Postmoderns are aware that they live in a morally complex world. They don't deal in absolutes and do understand that circumstances, upbringing, education, interactions with other people, and individual beliefs all play a part in what makes us who we are and how we live. That's not to say that there is no right or wrong. It's only to say that in some instances, the way we live may be neither right nor wrong, or may be shifting, or may be hard to understand.

Our Christian faith has a lot to offer these new generations in a world of postmodern moral ambiguity. Jesus commands us not to judge one another. In Luke 6:37-38, Jesus says, "Do not judge, and you will not be judged; do not condemn, and you will not be condemned. Forgive, and you will be forgiven; give, and it will be given to you. A good measure, pressed down, shaken together, running over, will be put into your lap; for the measure you give will be the measure you get back."

This passage is about living out the kingdom of God, about practicing Jesus' command to love God and love our neighbor. It's about the kind of relationships he wants us to have. When we judge each other, we build barriers and create walls, cutting off relationship. Instead, Jesus instructs us to forgive. When we encounter differences or difficulties with people and respond with forgiveness, we are drawn into closer relationship.

Judging others—and even judging ourselves—is part of the mechanism of sin, that which separates us from God and our neighbor. Judgment is the opposite of love. It is at the heart of the scapegoating system that I talked about in chapter 1. It's important to realize that Jesus commands us not to judge, because we are incapable of judging without self-interest. I judge people all the time, and it's not good for me. I judge people when I'm afraid, afraid they don't like me, afraid they are better than I am. I really judge people when it is

> **Is it possible to have an authentic relationship with someone who continues to act in ways that we consider sinful? Is it possible to love that person without judgment? Why or why not?**

obvious that they're better than me. If someone is a really good preacher, when their reading of the text is something completely new and profound, something I never thought of before, and their delivery is powerful and moving, I very often find fault with that person's hair or search for some slipup somewhere. Then I can't wait to find someone with whom to share my critique after the sermon. It's better if it's another minister, because that minister is more likely to join in the scapegoating with me. I judge people who drive Hummers. I point them out to my kids and say, "Look at that woman! She's driving a big gas-guzzler, and there's no one else in the car. Doesn't she know about global warming?" I've evidently done this quite a few times, because now my seven-year-old son points out the Hummers and SUVs and says, "Look, Papa, look at those people in that big car. Aren't they bad?" When he does that, I realize that I've taught him a way to bond with me by judging other people through scapegoating.

Blinding Judgment

Looking back at Saul, what leads him to such harsh judgment? He's a Pharisee and certainly has differences with other Jewish sects of his time, but there is something about the followers of Jesus, the Jewish Christians, that enrages him. Saul's judgmental zealotry is not based on his godlessness or his lack of righteousness or his ignorance of the Scriptures. No, it is just the opposite: His judgment is informed by his righteousness and knowledge of the law. Deuteronomy 21:22-23, says, "When someone is convicted of a crime punishable by death and is executed, and you hang him on a tree, his corpse must not remain all night upon the tree; you shall bury him that same day, for anyone hung on a tree is under God's curse."

Anyone hung on a tree is under God's curse. Jesus is convicted of a crime, is executed by crucifixion, is hung on a tree. Can you imagine the outrage? For Saul, a God-fearing literal believer of the law of God, to see someone who is clearly cursed by God being held up as the Messiah must be beyond intolerable.

In Acts 9, we see that Saul is driven. He snatches up his letters of authority and rushes at breakneck speed to Damascus, but he is stopped in his tracks. A bright, blinding light throws him to the ground. Before he can comprehend what has happened, he hears a voice saying, "Why are you persecuting me?"

"Who are you?" Saul asks, blind yet still searching.

"I am Jesus."

The object of his disdain, the very person responsible for the outbreak of this growing heretical movement and the spread of this perversion of God's law, has come to him, speaking as only God could. "Get up," Jesus says, "Go into the city, and you will be told what to do."

Saul—now Paul—gets uneasily to his feet. Blind and unsure of his footing, he has to be led into the city by his traveling companions. This humble, stumbling figure on the road is a stark contrast to the righteous and self-assured warrior of God thundering to Damascus. How could he have been so wrong? He was an observant Pharisee, which meant he spent time in prayer daily. He was a devoted student of the Torah, reading his Bible every day. He had dedicated his life to his faith and had believed with every fiber of his being that he was acting on the will of God. How did all that lead him to a rampaging persecution of the Messiah? Judgment is a tricky business. It can blind.

Paul has been confronted by Jesus. He is convinced, transformed. This is the come-to-Jesus meeting of all come-to-Jesus meetings. It seems remarkable that a man so convinced of his righteousness, so maniacal in his judgment, could experience such a radical transformation.

Judging Postmoderns

According to David Kinnaman's research, the new generations think that Christians are too judgmental. They're right; we are. And so are they, if they're human. But when Christians adopt a position of judgment and broadcast it loudly (and sometimes in the most hateful ways) in the marketplace, it is way too easy for people to see those messages as the totality of who we are. While Christians, like all people, are too judgmental, none of us are completely defined by our judgmental tendencies. I'm sure even that preacher who holds up the "I hate fags" signs loves his wife and kids. He's just like Saul of Tarsus; he is convinced by his reading of Scripture, by his passions, and by his prayers that his actions are the will of God. But also, and I think this applies to Saul as well, he probably feels threatened. He is threatened by something he can't completely understand, by something he vehemently disagrees with. It is okay to disagree on social issues from a biblical perspective. But the way those disagreements are voiced makes a difference. Differences should be communicated in the context of relationships. If the "I hate fags" guy approaches a homosexual with the desire to relate to that person with love and an attitude of forgiveness, those differences could be expressed and discussed in a way that would strengthen relationship and not sever it.

New generations live in a culture of moral ambiguity, and the gospel of Jesus Christ offers the perfect moral guide for this postmodern period. The moral and ethical guidelines of the gospel are not, at their core, black and white. Jesus teaches an ethic of love and relationship. The ethic of love and relationship can be appealed to in all situations. We can ask ourselves, "Am I acting out of love? Will this strengthen my relationship with God and with my neighbor? Or will it build barriers and sever my relationships?"

Postmoderns desire relationships. We worship a God who values relationship above all else. Postmoderns are less likely to judge one another based on differences in ideas, beliefs, or lifestyles, because diversity has been the norm for them. Perhaps there is a kind of faithfulness in the way the new generations tend to welcome diversity and value relationship over agreement. It is for the sake of relationship that God became human and entered our world. And when, instead of embracing God incarnate and responding to that invitation for relationship, humanity murdered Jesus, Jesus did not rise from the dead for retribution. Jesus defeated death, and in so doing, he made the cursed cross the sign of resurrection and his murder an act of reconciliation. We are judged by God, and God's judgment brings our sin out into the light, brings us out into the light where we can see the mercy of our Savior.

- nuChristians, like non-Christians, are too judgmental.
- nuChristians seek to respond in forgiveness and love for the sake of relationships.
- nuChristians believe that God is in Christ transforming them so that they might begin to live in noncompetitive, nonjudgmental relationships.
- nuChristians express differences and disagreements within the context of relationships.
- nuChristians are grateful for being judged with God's mercy.

CHAPTER 6

Sheltered from God's Children

"Those who worship vain idols forsake their true loyalty"
(Jonah 2:8).

Shelter Is Hard to Find

Are evangelical Christians too sheltered? David Kinnaman's research tells us that the new generations answer that question with a resounding yes. It is hard to believe that any of us could be sheltered today, even if we wanted to be. In contemporary culture, there is nearly complete saturation by media and communication technologies. There are twenty-four-hour news channels; twenty-four-hour movie and entertainment channels; twenty-four-hour weather channels; reality TV; home, garden, and fashion TV; sports and music channels; Spanish, Arabic, and a dozen other foreign-language TV channels. Any experience you're curious about or heavily into you can find among the hundreds of satellite and cable channels.

The Internet offers instant information about any subject matter that happens to cross your mind. If you want personal information about your favorite Indy-car driver, just google him. If you want the recipe for the best chili, google it. If you want to know what a kraken is, who the White Stripes are, or how many of the last five presidents were left-handed, google the question and find an answer.

You don't even need to go out searching for new information. If you buy a book on Amazon.com, the site will suggest ten others you might like. If you rent a movie on Netflix, the next time you log

In what ways do you think the evangelical church is too sheltered from the world? Might it ever be a good thing to be sheltered from a world run by a system that is often in contrast to the values of the kingdom of God? Why or why not?

on, you'll find a whole list of other movie suggestions. If you're on Facebook all day long, you're being fed new information about what people are doing, what books they're reading, which bands they're listening to, which political campaigns they support, which restaurants they eat in, which celebrities they follow, and what their kids are saying. Most websites and Facebook pages, even many e-mails, offer you not only text, but also audio and video.

With all this information about other people, new ideas, and different experiences coming at us constantly, how could anyone remain sheltered from the world?

Sheltered from Sin

Jonah was a good prophet. He was a righteous man of God. The Lord had called him and spoke to him. And in the book named for him, Jonah received a word from the Lord: "Go at once to Nineveh, that great city, and cry out against it; for their wickedness has come up before me" (Jonah 1:2).

Jonah was a good prophet—it is not like he got the word of the Lord wrong. But Jonah wanted nothing to do with the Ninevites. Nineveh was the capital city of Assyria, Israel's greatest enemy and eventual conqueror. They were wicked, vile people—enemies of God and Israel. He didn't want to expose himself to their perverted beliefs and practices. He wanted to see them punished, but he was worried that if he did go to Nineveh and cry out against them, there was a chance they would repent, and if they did, the Lord would have mercy on them. This possibility was more than Jonah could stomach.

This is the ancient equivalent to God coming to President Bush right after 9/11 and asking him to find Osama bin Laden so the

Lord could pardon bin Laden with divine mercy and love. So Jonah went in the opposite direction of Nineveh. He went to Joppa and got on a boat that he hoped would take him as far away as possible from the sinful city of Nineveh and its evil inhabitants.

Stepping from the Shelter

You might not have a Facebook or MySpace page, may not subscribe to Netflix or Rhapsody, may not read blogs, text from your phone, or tweet on Twitter, but the use of these services and technologies is nearly universal among postmodern generations. The new generations desire new experiences and new content constantly. The notion that someone would purposely limit exposure to other cultures, subcultures, lifestyles, or information would seem baffling to them.

There was once a time when conservative Christians deemed secular culture off-limits. They wouldn't go to movies or listen to non-Christian music and would limit their TV viewing to a few acceptable shows. Even among born-again Christians, the idea of limiting one's exposure to popular culture has largely gone by the wayside.

The shift is primarily due to Baby Boomer Christians' desire to break away from the strict limits of their parents' generation. At first they admired popular culture from afar, rejecting its content but imitating its form. They started Christian rock bands patterned after popular groups of the time. They opened Christian coffeehouses and music clubs to replicate the secular social scene, and they started all kinds of businesses with Christian angles to them.

We're in a period now where most Baby Boomer Christians and their children and, in some cases, their children's children, feel completely comfortable participating in what was once deemed secular popular culture. But while most Christians feel comfortable

---

Are righteousness and purity the same thing? Why or why not? To what extent is it possible to be in the world but not of it–to love it but not judge it?

63

consuming the same popular culture as their non-Christian cohorts, many Christians still remain intellectually sheltered.

Intellectually Sheltered but Culturally Exposed

Even though from my experience most Christians' cultural consumption patterns don't seem to be very different from their non-Christian peers, many of us still carry a sense of separation. We feel that we are somehow different, that we think differently and have different values. And in some areas, it's true. Many times I will talk to my mom or my sister after she has just seen the latest blockbuster movie, and when I ask how she liked it, she often will respond with something like, "I really liked it, but I don't know why they have to put so much sex in it," or "It was great, but every other word was a swear word."

This is a valid and reasonable response. It's a good thing to be able to enjoy a movie or a book and find meaning in it without having to embrace every part of it, even to find parts of it objectionable. But, the reaction can come from a kind of ideological schizophrenia. A person can enjoy fully participating in culture but at the same time possess a sense of judgment and even moral superiority. It's like thinking, "It's fine for me to see this movie, because I know the parts of it that are sinful or unhealthy." The implication is that the others, the outsiders, the non-Christians enjoy, pursue, or at the very least are not bothered by the graphic sex, violence, or over-the-top profanity. We need to understand that many of our Christian values are cultural values as well. Non-Christians of the same age seem to have similar moral values as Christians.

The one thing Christians and non-Christians *don't* have in common is a belief in Jesus Christ who came into the world to redeem it. John 3:17 says, "God did not send the Son into the world to condemn the world, but in order that the world might be saved through him." That verse might suggest some ways that nuChristians should respond to the world. First of all, we are called into the

> **What cultural values have their roots in Judeo-Christian tradition? In contrast, what so-called Christian values have their roots in capitalist, democratic, American culture?**

world (i.e., popular/secular culture) and are to enter it without judgment. We can engage culture without completely endorsing it. And if we hope to reach postmodern generations, it will be necessary to understand the culture and subcultures they live in.

I was recently at a church growth conference, and two different speakers spent a significant amount of time talking about the importance of door knocking. They explained how a new church planter should get a map of the zip codes surrounding their new church and go street by street, knocking on every single door and inviting the residents to their new church. In the entire three-day conference, outreach via the Internet was not mentioned once. This is another example of Christian cultural schizophrenia. I'm sure the leaders of the conference use e-mail and check out websites to get information about new businesses or restaurants before they go, and they would probably greet a stranger knocking at their own door with suspicion. When it comes to planting a church, however, they revert to strategies and tactics from another time. Many Christians engage culture one way on a personal level, but when it comes to the church or their faith, they respond very differently. (Even the typical church website tends to be a static, informational page that plays little significant role in the ministry life and outreach of the congregation.)

For most new visitors to House of Mercy, their first stop is not the church building but the church website. More people visit our website every day than attend worship on Sunday. More people listen to our sermons online than listen to them while sitting in the pews. I get e-mails from people all the time asking questions about the church after they have visited our website. I'm able to communicate with visitors before they even show up at church. After answering their questions via e-mail, I ask them to be sure to come and introduce themselves to me if they decide to visit our church in person. When they do, I already know their names and something about them.

Called into the World

In ignoring God's call into the ungodly city, Jonah was not just fleeing an unpleasant calling. No, he was fleeing from the Lord (Jonah 1:3), a fact he freely confessed to the sailors on board the boat (1:10). The incredible thing is that the Lord went after him. The Lord didn't just get another prophet to do his will; the Lord does not just go save the Ninevites through a supernatural invention. Of course, the Lord didn't *need* Jonah in order to show mercy to Nineveh; God wanted Jonah to go to into that worldly city.

God wanted Jonah to go—but Jonah decided he would rather die. He had the sailors throw him overboard in the middle of the ocean. Notice that he could have repented of his reluctance and avoidance and said, "I am sorry, Lord. I will do what you ask (if you will just calm the storm and spare all of our lives)." Instead, he told the sailors, "Pick me up and throw me into the sea" (Jonah 1:12).

But being rather fond of Jonah, God had a great fish swallow him and spit him back on the shore where he had started. The Lord said to Jonah, "Get up, go to Nineveh, that great city, and proclaim to it the message that I tell you" (Jonah 3:2).

So Jonah went not because he had changed his mind or had learned compassion for the godless—he just figured he didn't have a choice. Once you try to drown yourself in the middle of the ocean, and a fish carries you in its belly for three days and deposits you back on shore, you just figure there is no way you are getting away. When the Lord is after you, well, you're going to get caught.

Jonah therefore went to the capital city of his nation's enemy, into the heart of the ungodly world, and did what the Lord asked him to do. Not that he really embraced the spirit of the task. He went into the middle of the city and said, "Forty days more, and Nineveh shall be overthrown!" (Jonah 3:4). Not really much of a sermon. Far from a compassionate and wholehearted plea to inspire repentance. It wasn't much—but it was enough. The whole city responded and repented. The king puts on sackcloth and ashes, and everyone, even the animals, fasted in the hope that God would show them mercy.

> When God saw what they did, how they turned from their evil ways, God changed his mind about the calamity that he had said he would bring upon them; and he did not do it. But this was very displeasing to Jonah, and he became angry. He prayed to the LORD and said, "O LORD! Is not this what I said while I was still in my own country? That is why I fled to Tarshish at the beginning; for I knew that you are a gracious God and merciful, slow to anger, and abounding in steadfast love, and ready to relent from punishing. And now, O LORD, please take my life from me, for it is better for me to die than to live." And the LORD said, "Is it right for you to be angry?" Then Jonah went out of the city and sat down east of the city, and made a booth for himself there. He sat under it in the shade, waiting to see what would become of the city. (Jonah 3:10–4:5)

Jonah watched what would happen, hoping against hope that he was wrong about the Lord and that he would get to see some classic "slaying of thine enemies."

But it didn't happen, because not only was the Lord fond of Jonah, but the Lord liked the Ninevites. They repented; they were saved by the mercy of the Lord; they were brought into the love of God. And it seems clear to me that this is the reason God didn't just find another prophet or do the call-to-repentance thing by the

> This chapter's title is "Sheltered from God's Children." What does that title suggest to you in light of Jonah's story? How might our own tendencies to shelter ourselves from the world hinder us in doing God's work?

Spirit alone—the Lord wanted Jonah to be there. The Lord didn't send Jonah just so the Ninevites would change. God wanted *Jonah* to change, to leave his sheltered life and enter the wider world so he could see that God's love and mercy are for all God's children.

Cultural Relevance vs. Cultural Literacy

Despite the very real schizophrenia I see in Christians today, I have also observed a majority move away from past generations' reluctance to engage secular culture. In fact, it seems to me that even while many Christian churches still preach against overexposure to popular culture's values and influence, they also worry about being too out of touch with that culture. I perceive a great fear among contemporary Christian leaders that our churches are not being culturally relevant.

Everybody wants to be culturally relevant—relevant worship, relevant preaching, relevant music. The consultants say that if you are not culturally relevant, then you will not be able to reach the new generations. Reaching the new generations is what every church that is interested in growing wants to do.

Among many Christians, there is this embarrassment about just how old our faith is. It is, like, so old, like thousands of years old. And the Christian church is so old. The buildings are so old; the songs are so old. And old is bad. Old is irrelevant. So the preacher gets an ear pierced and grows a goatee. This, my friend, was a very hip and culturally relevant thing to do, cutting edge even—in 1985. And that is the problem with making cultural relevance a priority. To speak to the "young people" on the cutting edge of popular culture by imitating them is like chasing a wave on a bicycle. The wave keeps moving and then disappears, and you are left trying to ride a bike underwater.

The edge keeps moving. The *now* is the *then* by the time you ever hear about it.

In contemporary Christian leadership magazines, I have actually read vocabulary lists of the current slang, with suggestions on how to use the terms in a sermon. You know, so you can relate to the "young people." I heard a sermon by a preacher, who, I think, had just recently taken off his tie and bought a cordless mic. I am pretty sure that he had read the same article I had. He held the microphone up to his mouth like an upside-down ice cream cone and shouted into it, "What's up, 'Holmes boy'!" This from a forty-year-old white guy. It was not a moment of cultural relevance. It was more like a greeting from Dr. Watson.

The twentieth-century Swiss theologian Karl Barth says a preacher should aim beyond the hills of relevance. You see, our faith is old, but it is also timeless. If a preacher preaches for the now, she or he limits the truth, makes it tiny and insignificant. A church that is focused on the Good News of Jesus has something timeless to offer. Speculating that if Jesus returned today, he would broadcast the Sermon on the Mount via Twitter and calling his disciples by posting a video on YouTube might be a stab at cultural relevance, but it is not proclaiming the timeless Good News of Jesus.

There is a difference between cultural relevance and cultural literacy. It is a good thing to understand popular culture. It is not such a good thing to imitate popular culture merely as a way to sell Jesus to people, because that is how everyone sells everything. The more you use the methods of Madison Avenue to position Jesus in the culture

> **From a Christian perspective, what is morally or ethically neutral in culture? Or does the Christian faith have something to say about every aspect of our lives? Why or why not?**

market, the more people come to see Jesus as just another culture product. And they take Jesus as seriously as they do any other product. People don't usually give their lives to products. Products hardly ever reconcile the world to God and usher in the age of Jubilee.

Being culturally literate, being part of the world that God loves and that Jesus came to reconcile, requires only that you be aware of the world you live in. You don't have to imitate it to engage it. To understand popular culture is helpful in understanding the context in which the Good News is being heard. In the same way, understanding first-century Palestinian culture is helpful for understanding the context in which the Good News was first proclaimed by the apostles. Only by understanding and engaging today's culture can we transform it and, in turn, be transformed by the Lord's plan for the rest of God's children.

The new generations revel in expanding their exposure to the whole wide world. They do not proceed with fear that they will be tarnished, but with an expectation that their lives will be enriched and their understanding widened. The gospel is all about an ever-expanding circle of grace. Perhaps we can let these new generations be our guides in this new world in which we are not completely fluent, and they will help us to learn more about what it means to love the world. In the same way, God called Jonah to Nineveh, not for God's sake nor even just for the sake of the Ninevites, but for Jonah's benefit as well, that he might see the breadth of who God's children are and the depth of God's love and mercy.

■ nuChristians live in the world with love, not judgment.
■ nuChristians are culturally literate.
■ nuChristians are eager to engage the breadth and depth of all of God's children.
■ nuChristians understand that they are influenced by culture in the same ways that non-Christians are.
■ nuChristians engage and influence culture.

CHAPTER 7

The Politics of Reconciliation

*"As he came out of the temple, one of his disciples said to him,
'Look, Teacher, what large stones and what large buildings!'"*
(Mark 13:1).

Too Political

When new generations charge that Christians are too political, I don't think they are objecting to our general involvement in the democratic process. Christians have been intricately involved in politics since the founding of our nation. Politicians in every office imaginable, from members of local school boards, mayors, and governors, to congressional representatives, senators, and U.S. presidents approach their duties from a place of deeply held Christian convictions. The most successful have done so with the understanding that politics is the art of compromise. Pastors, archbishops, lay leaders, and Christian individuals have acted successfully from outside elected government office to influence our political process in ways that have greatly benefited our cities, states, and nation. However, when individuals and organizations enter the political arena, not seeking a dialogue but issuing demands, the postmodern person raises an eyebrow.

Until recently, the most prominent Christian leaders in politics were nearly all aligned with the very conservative wing of the Republican Party, practicing the politics of "Us versus Them" and using speech that divided people, derided people, and made dialogue

> **How do we blur the lines between patriotism and faith? How can we keep these ideas separate and in the right order of priority?**

nearly impossible. This kind of insistence on seeing issues as black and white, as absolutely morally right or wrong, with no room for compromise and no willingness to consider the positions of the other, is antithetical to the postmodern mind-set.

To demonize a person or a group of people because they don't agree with you is a kind of judgmental dishonesty. Ted Kennedy, Rush Limbaugh, John McCain, or Barack Obama cannot be the kind of heartless incarnations of evil as those in extreme opposition to them charge. Charges of "baby killer," "pervert," "God-hater," "anti-American," or any number of reductive epithets are not only ugly, they are not true. New-generation Americans understand that a person's given position on a single issue does not define that person completely, even if that position is the opposite of the listener's political or moral priorities.

It seems to me that the problem isn't that Christians are too political; it may be that they're not political enough. The Christian political spokespeople who make the most noise and have received the most media coverage are not engaged in true politics, but in incendiary ideological rhetoric.

Faith and/or Politics

In Mark's story of Jesus, the disciples love politics. Time after time, they demonstrate their misunderstanding of what the new kingdom that Jesus comes to usher in is all about. They're living in a country that was once, in the distant past, a mighty political power and is now occupied by the armies of Rome. They have grown up with the promise that one day the Messiah will come and restore Israel to its greatness. They think they've found this Messiah when they find Jesus. After Jesus invites them into his inner circle, they begin to entertain visions not only of Israel's return to power, but of their own rise as powerful political insiders.

In the second half of the book, beginning with Mark 8:22, we see the disciples and Jesus becoming more at odds, as Jesus begins to speak about his death and the disciples seek reassurance about their longed-for positions of political power.

The section leading up to Jesus' entry into Jerusalem begins and ends with Jesus healing two blind men. Mark uses these miracles as a set of bookends to emphasize the blindness of the disciples, as demonstrated by their actions following the healing of the blind man at Bethsaida and preceding the healing of blind Bartimaeus. These two men, who were blind to the kingdom of God, were given sight by Jesus and responded with faith. In contrast, Jesus' disciples, whom he had taught the secrets of the kingdom of God, had become blind to the Good News, blinded by their own ambition.

After healing the first blind man, Jesus and his disciples set out on their way. As they were walking, Jesus asked them about what the people were saying about him. And after the disciples answered, Jesus asked them, "But who do you say that I am?" (Mark 8:29). Peter answered on behalf of the disciples, proclaiming that Jesus is the Messiah. Jesus warned them not to tell anyone. This seems like an odd response on Jesus' part, unless you consider that he knew that what the disciples meant by Messiah was very different from the kind of Messiah he was. In an attempt to clarify his mission, he told them he must go to Jerusalem and be rejected by everyone, be condemned by the elders and the chief priests, be killed and after three days rise again.

Peter took Jesus aside and rebuked him. Jesus responded by telling Peter that his mind was not on divine things but on human things. Jesus was making the point that Peter and the disciples seemed to be more interested in a political kingdom than in the kingdom of God.

A chapter later, in Mark 9:30, Jesus again tried to explain to the disciples the kind of Messiah he is, saying, "The Son of Man is to be betrayed into human hands, and they will kill him, and three days after being killed, he will rise again." But they did not understand what he was talking about and were afraid to ask him. The disciples quickly moved on to talking about something else; they began arguing. So, when they reached their destination, Jesus asked them what they had been arguing about. They didn't say anything, because they had been arguing about which one of them was the most important. They were already fighting over cabinet posts in what they imagined was going to be Jesus' new administration!

Beginning in Mark 10:32, Jesus tried to explain it for a third time. He took the twelve disciples aside and said to them, "See, we are going up to Jerusalem, and the Son of Man will be handed over to the chief priests and the scribes, and they will condemn him to death; then they will hand him over to the Gentiles; they will mock him, and spit upon him, and flog him, and kill him; and after three days he will rise again."

This would have been pretty shocking if you were expecting Jesus to go into Jerusalem, throw the Roman soldiers out, and take his place as the rightful king of Israel. But in order for this to shock the listener, that listener would have to be paying attention to what Jesus was saying. The disciples weren't paying attention. They were so taken with their understanding of what they believed the kingdom of God would be, they couldn't even hear Jesus' words. There would be no political power; there *would* be suffering and sacrifice, but that fact seemed to go right by them. They were concerned with other matters. In fact, after Jesus finished telling them about his torture, execution, and resurrection, James and John came forward and said to Jesus, "Teacher, we want you to do for us whatever we ask of you" (Mark 10:35). Jesus asked them, "What is it you want me to do for you?" Then the two brothers went on to tell Jesus that they wanted him to guarantee that they would get the number two and number three positions in the new world order. Anticipating that Jesus was about to take the throne in Jerusalem, they wanted to be sitting on his right and on his left.

> **To what extent do we have trouble seeing the difference between politics and faith? How can we participate in the political arena in ways that bear witness to the mercy of Jesus Christ?**

After this incident, they came across a second blind man on the road calling out to Jesus. Jesus asked blind Bartimaeus the same question he had just asked James and John, "What do you want me to do for you?" (Mark 10:51). But unlike James and John, the blind man did not ask for power; he asked for mercy and healing. The blind man asked to see. Jesus replied him that his faith has made him well, and Mark writes, "Immediately [Bartimaeus] regained his sight and followed him on the way" (10:52). This is almost the exact language that Mark uses to describe the first disciples Jesus calls: Peter, Andrew, James, and John: "And immediately they left their nets and followed him" (Mark 1:18).

The Two Kingdoms

The true nature of the political process in a democracy is one of well intentioned citizens of varying backgrounds and beliefs coming together to form policies and laws in the interest of the common good. In America, as in Christianity, we are also charged to protect the rights and well-being of the minority, the outsider, to give a voice to the voiceless, to empower the powerless, and to help those who cannot help themselves. That definition is almost shocking when we consider that the politics we observe today seem to have very little in common with that task.

It is not just Christians who have chosen the politics of scapegoating, fear, hate, and incendiary ideological rhetoric over collaboration for the common good. The politics we observe look more like two parties playing a very high-stakes game for power and control. This kind of politics guarantees that there are very few winners and that the losers are the majority of the American people. NuChristians need to be involved in politics in ways that bear wit-

> In what ways do our political preferences contradict our theological convictions? How do we bend our biblical understanding to support our political convictions?

ness to the reconciling love of Jesus Christ. When Paul writes in 2 Corinthians 5:19 "in Christ God was reconciling the world to himself, not counting their trespasses against them, and entrusting the message of reconciliation to us," the apostle is not only talking about reconciling individuals to God, but also about giving us a ministry of reconciling individuals one to another. Instead of contributing to the politics of division and power grabbing, nuChristians have the ability to reorient the political process. Instead of following the example of the kingdom of the world, we need to bring the values of the kingdom of God into politics. We can work to heal, to reconcile those who think it's necessary to vilify the opposition in order to protect their own position.

Instead, it seems like the most vocal Christian leaders in politics are the worst offenders when it comes to divisive rhetoric and entrenched positions. A good example of this is the controversy that arose over displaying the Ten Commandments in public parks, schools, and courthouses. Church leaders were all over the news, claiming that the rights of Christians and the foundational beliefs of Christianity were being threatened. Their claim was that the removal of an object, a monument, or a plaque, could somehow threaten or diminish the deeply held beliefs of Christianity. These claims seem to me to come from a lack of faith.

We are not different from non-Christians in that we have a tendency to go on the offensive when our beliefs are challenged. It's a basic human instinct. We respond that way partly as a survival mechanism, but also as a way of reassuring ourselves that the beliefs we hold are true. We've learned from being born and raised in the kingdom of the world that someone else's opposing ideas or beliefs diminish our own. This is the scapegoating mechanism at work again. We are afraid—and such fear is an expression of our lack of faith—so we find others who are afraid of the same thing, and we pick an enemy. We dehumanize the enemy and accuse them of all kinds of evil. This mechanism reassures us. It's not *us* that might be wrong or weak; it's *them*. They are responsible for our fear, doubt, and uncertainty. If we can get rid of them, ostracize them, annihilate them, figuratively or literally, then we will be okay. And our faith is affirmed. Faith, however, is not dependent on finding scapegoats or on public displays. We need never worry about our faith being taken from us by powers and principalities. Faith is a gift from the Holy Spirit—the same Spirit whose work is evidenced by acts of inclusion and reconciliation, not division.

The average white, middle-class, evangelical Christian should not be worried about defending his or her own rights. We have no need to defend ourselves. White middle-class Christians are the best-represented group in America, politically and in every other way! Racial minorities, the poor, the underemployed, and those of other religious traditions are the people who are vastly underrepresented in our government. We are called to be the servants of all, not the protectors of our own self-interests. We have Good News to bring to the government, a gospel of love and reconciliation, that when acted upon, puts the rights of underrepresented groups before our own.

Let's imagine a scenario where the postmodern generations are heard to say things like, "Christians are always concerned about other people. They are always working for the underprivileged. They're at the forefront of every movement concerned with the rights of others. Christians give power away and are always working to bring people together." Doesn't that sound like the fulfillment of what Jesus declared: "By this everyone will know that you are my disciples, if you have love for one another" (John 13:34-35)?

The postmodern landscape is not made up of ideas and issues with only two possible positions. The new generations don't feel obligated to come down on either one side or the other, nor do they feel that one's position must remain static. They see the possibility of many ways to look at an issue and the possibility that one's position can change based on experience, more information, or the desire to compromise. Relationships are seen as more important than political positions. If the real heart of Christianity, with its emphasis on relationships and its ethic of love, were understood, postmoderns would find it very attractive and in line with many of their own values.

Called to See beyond the Political

The next section of Mark's Gospel is structured around three visits to the temple. Jesus and his followers finally reached Jerusalem but did not enter the city. Instead, they stayed just outside at Bethany. Jesus sent two of his disciples to get the requisite donkey for his entrance, commonly known as the triumphal entry. But unlike other Gospels, in Mark it was not much of a triumph. The whole city did not come out to greet them as Matthew describes in his Gospel. It was only those who were traveling with him who laid their cloaks and some leafy branches on the road in front of Jesus. (That's right: leafy branches cut from the nearby fields. Mark does not specify palm branches, and there is not even any waving.) The group of people, headed by the disciples, paved the road with what they could find nearby and shouted, "Blessed is the coming kingdom of our ancestor David!" (Mark 11:10).

Only in Mark's Gospel is this point made so clearly. The kingdom that the disciples and other followers were heralding was not the kingdom of God, but a political kingdom. It was the restoration of the kingdom of David.

In contrast, Jesus took his disciples into the temple three times over the next three days, teaching not that the power and authority of the nation of Israel would be restored, with Jerusalem and the temple as its center, but that the temple had been corrupted. The house of God had been turned into a house of thieves. Jesus interrupted business as usual in the temple. He threw out the

> What political issues and controversies distract us and detract from the gospel of Jesus? How can we avoid such distractions and detractions while still remaining engaged in transforming the kingdom of the world into the kingdom of God?

money changers and forbade those working in the sacrifice business to continue their tasks.

Over the next two days, Jesus challenged the authorities in their elevation of the political kingdom over the kingdom of God. He told them to give to Caesar what belongs to Caesar, but give to God what is God's. He reminded them that the laws that supersede all others are to love God first and to love one's neighbor. As an example of one who lives out the laws, Jesus pointed not to the powerful priests, but to the lowly widow giving up all that she had.

After all these teachings, did the disciples finally understand that the kingdom that Jesus would usher in was not a stronger political entity, but the kingdom of God, which stands in opposition to the ways of the kingdoms of the world? Leaving the temple for the final time, one of the disciples stopped, looked admiringly and with awe at the impressive structure of the temple, and said to Jesus, "Look, Teacher, what large stones and what large buildings!" (Mark 13:1). After all Jesus had taught them, it was still the physical display of power that impressed the disciples, not the beauty of the poor widow who gave everything nor the call to active love. It was not too long after this that Jesus was betrayed and abandoned by his followers.

The Politics of the Gospel

The House of Mercy members, like many postmoderns, are very politically involved. Some of them are elected officials; some have served as delegates at the recent political conventions; and some work lobbying state and local government on behalf of educational, nonprofit, and social service agencies. Our definition of *political* is very broad. We see actions that serve others, that work for reconciliation in communities, and that strengthen families and communities as political actions.

In addition to past involvement in the Joint Religious Legislative Coalition (an organization that trains people to lobby state government on issues of poverty, justice, and the environment), we are also involved with the Whole Farm Co-op. The Co-op is made up of family farmers and small manufacturers who produce meats, cheeses, grains, vegetables, soaps, lumber, and household items. They are all dedicated to organic and sustainable practices. They have a program called "congregational-based agriculture". We buy directly from the producers, ordering online, and the co-op delivers once a month to the church. This is not only a way for people in the congregation to get the best quality food produced in ways that are healthiest for the environment, the land, and the animals, but it also provides a way for family farmers to stay on their land. It builds community among the farmers and between the farmers and the urban congregations they serve. Several times a year, the farms have open houses, so we can see where our food comes from and get to know the people who grow it for us. Their slogan is "Change the world one meal at the time." I believe that's the kind of political action that puts the Christian ethic of love and the ministry of reconciliation to work. It is the kind of political action that the new generations *do* value.

■ nuChristians are involved in the political process.

■ nuChristians seek political dialogue and build relationships across political boundaries.

■ nuChristians enter the political arena with the values of the kingdom of God.

■ nuChristians work to establish and protect the rights of the powerless, those whom Jesus called "the least of these."

■ nuChristians, like non-Christians and the first Christians, have internalized the values of the kingdom of the world and fail much of the time to live out the values of the kingdom of God.

CHAPTER 8

Continuing the Conversation

My dad has been a Baptist minister for more than forty years. In that time, he has seen several major generational and cultural shifts in America. Over the years, he has tried to communicate the gospel in ways that could best be understood at the particular time and place in which he has found himself. In the late '60s in Southern California, he took a dying urban church and began ministering to the growing counterculture. He used music, art, and theater to draw in *that* new generation and to proclaim the gospel.

In the 1970s, he started a house-based church in the Midwest and tapped into the Me Generation's desire for self-discovery. His church used small encounter groups, retreats, and workshops to help seekers understand how life in Christ was the ultimate destination of the inward journey. In the '80s, he moved to the desert Southwest and followed the conservative turn in the nation, building a congregation of seventy people into a six hundred–member, full-service-program church with a family life center, a gym, a swimming pool, and a restaurant. Since the mid-'90s, he has been ministering to Slavic immigrants in Portland, Oregon, specializing in working with their young adults as they try to make the adjustment to American culture and American Christianity.

With all his experience working with several different new generations and being part of one of the last generations to grow up in the complete cultural context of modernism, I thought it could be insightful to ask him to read what I have been writing and to have a conversation with him about it. So, I sent him the manuscript, and we arranged a phone call.

ME: Hey, Dad. Well, maybe we could start out by talking about some of your general impressions and see where the conversation goes.

DAD: Sounds good.

ME: So, what are your general impressions?

DAD: Well, first of all, I like your emphasis on kingdom living, and I can say more about that later. Also, I have to say that we have some clear theological differences.

ME: Yeah, I was expecting that might come up.

DAD: I think there are some things that are clear in the Bible, and while there are many things that are open to interpretation, there are some that are not.

ME: Is there one in particular you would like to talk about?

DAD: Okay, how about salvation? I think it is important to be clear with people that God loves them and offers them salvation. Knowing that there are consequences for rejecting that offer does motivate people. And I am not talking about a hell that is fire and brimstone and eternal torture, but an eternity in the complete absence of God.

ME: Do you want to say any more about theological differences?

DAD: Do you want me to?

ME: How about we move on? I am sure they are bound to come up in the conversation.

DAD: Okay.

ME: Do you think that the new generations, the Mosaics and Busters, as some call them, are significantly different than other new generations?

DAD: It seems like every new generation reacts in some way to the generation that comes before them. We saw that in the '60s with the Hippie culture. When we moved to Ventura, [California], there was really a lot going on. There were some exciting things going on.

Kids were expressing themselves in very creative ways. They were kind of looking for a sense of freedom. They didn't really want to go to college and become businessmen just because it was expected of them.

When I first went to Bethel Baptist, I did what I would do at every other church I was called to. I looked around and saw who wasn't going to church—and there, it was almost everyone but the few old saints of the church that had been there all along. What really struck me, though, was there were absolutely none of the high school- and college-age kids that were such a vibrant part of the city and the culture all around the church.

ME: Vibrant? Is that how everyone saw them?

DAD: Well, no. You know, people thought they were "long hairs" and didn't bathe and had no respect and didn't have jobs. A lot of people thought they were troublemakers. But I thought, these are really the people that this church needs—they are what is missing from this church. And I thought their energy and their creativity had a lot to offer the church.

So I got to know them. I just started going were they were. I figured out what they liked and what was important to them. I asked them to do things like come and play their music for us in the church or offer art lessons or candle making in the church's basement. Whatever they were exploring, I offered to help if I could, to be a part of it if I could. Of course, there were a lot of things that their freedom got them into that weren't so good, and I tried to help them with that, too. I worked with a lot of kids to get [them] off drugs and got to know the parents of kids with troubled family lives, brought runaways home.

ME: So, did these kids start coming to church?

DAD: Oh yeah. We started a Christian coffeehouse in the church basement, and a lot of them came there first and then started coming Sunday mornings. They participated a lot in the service. They would read poetry and play their guitars. We started singing different music than just the traditional hymns. They really brought a lot to the church.

ME: Did many of them become Christians?

DAD: Yeah, we would go down to the beach and baptize them. But back to your question about the difference with the new generations, what you call "postmoderns" a lot in your writing. I think they are the same as previous new generations in that they are doing things differently than, say, their parents' generation, but I also think there are some real differences.

ME: What would you say are the main differences?

DAD: They do seem like they have a kind of moral relativity that is different. It is like anything anyone wants to do is fine. I think it is important to be clear that there are truths in the Bible that are absolute, and things that are right and wrong. And I think, as a minister, I need to be up front about that, but not necessarily in a challenging way. You start by getting to know them and model the kingdom of God, like you are saying. You start with "God loves you" and go from there.

ME: Do you think your strategy of seeing who is missing from the church and then going out and finding them, getting to know them, and then inviting them to bring who they are into the church will work as well with postmoderns as it has with other generations that you've worked with?

DAD: I think there are a lot of people who are missing from the church, and it is not hard to find them. Yes, then you get to know them and invite them in. I do wonder, though, if the new generations might be a little harder.

ME: How come?

DAD: Well, first of all, I don't really know them, so it is harder to say. I haven't spent a lot of time working with these generations. I work with kids this age, but they are Slavic immigrants, and they are coming from a different culture and a much more conservative culture. One thing that I worry about, though, from talking to you and doing some reading, and reading what you wrote...

ME: What is it?

DAD: It seems that there are a lot of differences. In some ways you are saying to be able to reach out and minister to these new generations, I have to change my theology.

ME: I don't think I am saying that.

DAD: It sounds like it. I have to change what I think about homosexuality, abortion, politics, the Bible, salvation...[*laughs*]... about the belief in absolute truth.

ME: That does seem like a lot of things. But I am not saying that you have to change what you think about these things. I am just suggesting what I think most postmoderns think about these subjects. And I am not trying to suggest that they all think the same way on any particular subject. I am trying to talk more about how they think or how they approach things. It is more about tolerance. Which means there is room for all kinds of difference. It doesn't matter if someone is gay, straight, black, white, Iraqi, or even a Baptist minister. That is not what matters; what matters is being honestly, authentically you, and allowing other people to be honestly, authentically who they are. I would say two really important ideas are tolerance and authenticity.

DAD: As long as tolerance isn't really just "anything anyone wants to do and believe is fine."

ME: Well, it is saying that anything anyone wants to do and believe is fine—I mean I am not talking about hurting other people or themselves—but it is fine for those people who do and believe those things. It doesn't have to be fine for you. You don't have to change or do or think what they do or think. That is the point of postmodernity; we all bring different things to the conversation, but everyone gets to have a voice in the conversation. It also doesn't mean that it is necessarily a Christian conversation. We reserve places where we have Christian conversations, like on Sunday mornings or Bible studies. That doesn't mean if someone doesn't agree with what is being said, they are not welcome. We should just try to be clear about what we are doing on a Sunday and why we are doing it, so people who are not Christians can understand it and feel welcome.

DAD: Well, this is all very interesting. It is different than saying, "This is the Truth, and we know it, and if you want to know the Truth, you have to accept it." Is it more like saying, "This is what is the Truth for me, and yours may be different"?

ME: Kind of. It is saying that, but ultimately believing that God is in Christ reconciling the world to God's self. I really believe that the Holy Spirit comes to people, God's creation, and convicts them in a way they eventually cannot resist. The Holy Spirit was able to give me the gift of faith. Why am I any different than anyone else? All will come to the Father through the Son. It might not happen tomorrow; it might happen at the end of time, but—

DAD: I raised a Universalist [*laughs*].

ME: Well, you raised a Baptist minister who grew up in the post-modern age [*laughs*]. Thanks a lot for taking the time to read what I have been thinking about and talk to me about it.

DAD: It was fun and interesting. You want to say hi to Mom?

ME: Sure.

Finding Faith in a New Generation

The postmodern generations do see the world in some very different ways than do generations influenced by modernity, but the way in which they are the same overwhelms those differences. They are created children of God; they are humans. That is the overwhelming commonality shared by Christians, nuChristians, and non-Christians alike. We are humans living in a place whose values, laws, morals, and ethics are formed by the kingdom of this world. To put it in a way my dad might say it, we are all fallen people living in a fallen world.

The beautiful thing is that that is not the end of the story. We know God through Christ, and we know God to be full of mercy and love. Our tendencies to be hypocritical, only interested in reinforcing our own perspectives, intolerant, sheltered, too political, and judgmental are some of the common traits of fallen humans. These are traits shared by some of the heroes of the Bible, and God loved them and used them anyway. Abraham and Sarah, Isaac and Rebekah, Jacob, Rachel, and Leah, Moses and Miriam, David, Naaman, Jonah, Peter, all the disciples, all non-Christians, and all nuChristians are loved by God. It is not necessary for us to worry about our reputations with non-Christians, or even to worry about the way we tarnish Jesus' reputation. Jesus never really had a very good reputation with people who rejected his message. There is a difference, you see, between worrying about reputations and just living out the commandment to love God and one another.

The gospel of Jesus Christ is for all people for all time. In postmodernity, we have the opportunity to bring the gospel to new generations who are receptive to its message of unconditional love and forgiveness, of tolerance and inclusion, of the ethic of love over legalism, of reconciliation over divisiveness, of a concern for the poor over the powerful. When we proceed with humility and passion, seeking authentic relationships of love, flowing from the love of God, I think we will find new generations longing for the particularity of the Christian faith.

When non-Christians observe that the lives of Christians look more like their own lives, they are right. They look like human lives: messy, hypocritical, self-interested, judgmental, competitive, but they are also loving, compassionate, vulnerable, hopeful, and seeking relationship. What is different is the nuChristians' faith in God, who calls us to another way, a way of ever-expanding grace, built on love and the transforming work of Jesus Christ. On this way we find life, and that abundantly.

- nuChristians listen to and consider the opinions of others.
- nuChristians try to love others, even when others reject their beliefs.
- nuChristians' lives are admittedly flawed.
- nuChristians know that human perfection is an illusion.
- nuChristians believe that the conversation itself is important and should continue.

Finding Faith in the New Generation of the Black Church

FROM JAY-Z TO JESUS:
Reaching & Teaching Young Adults in the Black Church

Benjamin Stephens and Ralph C. Watkins; Foreword by Otis Moss III

"Dr. Watkins and Rev. Stephens offer church leaders insights and guidelines for developing a relevant and inviting ministry that will reintroduce this generation, who already know Jay-Z intimately, to a different and better role model, Jesus Christ."
—from the foreword by Otis Moss III, senior pastor, Trinity United Church of Christ

"*From Jay-Z to Jesus* offers a common sense approach with practical applications on how to really engage young adults in ministry for the 21st-century black church and beyond."
—Cheryl L. Walker, director of African American Ministries, General Board of Discipleship of The United Methodist Church

"*From Jay-Z to Jesus* will help the reader build an effective ministry to young adults that will minister to their needs as well as disciple them to be leaders in the church and community. Every leader in the church should read this book."
—*CBA Retailers + Resources*, April 2009

"I highly recommend this book for churches, educators and pastors. Seminaries would do well to use it somewhere in Pastoral Theology."

—Dr. Frazier N. Odom, interim executive director,
The Lutheran Church Missouri Synod

"In this brief but powerful book, I was both startled and awakened to alternative approaches to ministry among my peers."

—Rev. Charlton L. Johnson, vice president,
Connectional Young Adult Ministry

"The authors offer helpful insights into teaching this generation including personal stories written by young adults themselves. This is a very useful book, particularly for those working in church-based contexts."

—*Campus Ministry Update*, April 2009

978-0-8170-1545-9 $15.00

To order, call 800-458-3766
or visit www.judsonpress.com.

JUDSON PRESS
PUBLISHERS SINCE 1824

VISIT Russell Rathbun's Blog!

Post-Rapture: Lost Writings
from a Failed Revolution

The Reverend Richard Lamblove is
the sometimes semi-fictional persona
of Reverend Russell Rathbun, the
author of *NuChristian: Finding
Faith in a New Generation*, *Post-
Rapture Radio: Lost Writings from
a Failed Revolution* and *Midrash on the Juanitos*, whose main
character is also Rev. Lamblove.

Post-Rapture serves to provide a further place for the Reverend to write about the Bible, culture, preaching and perception theory.

http://revlamblove.wordpress.com/